AS-Level
History

Russia in Revolution (1881-1924)
From Autocracy to Dictatorship

There's a lot to learn if you're studying AS-Level History.

Luckily, this book takes you through everything you need to know for Unit 1, Option D3, with plenty of analysis to help you see why things happened the way they did. Plus, it's got loads of practice questions to test your knowledge.

It also has a whole section on how to turn what you've learnt into a top-notch exam answer, to help you prepare for the big day.

And of course, we've done our best to make the whole thing vaguely entertaining for you.

Complete Revision and Practice
Exam Board: Edexcel (Unit 1, Option D3)

Published by CGP

Editors:
David Broadbent, Polly Cotterill, Luke von Kotze, Holly Poynton

Contributors:
Peter Callaghan, Vanessa Musgrove

Proofreaders:
Hugh Mascetti, Glenn Rogers

Acknowledgements

With thanks to Mary Evans Picture Library for permission to use the images on pages 7, 19, 24 & 30

ISBN: 978 1 84762 674 5

Groovy Website: www.cgpbooks.co.uk

Printed by Elanders Ltd, Newcastle upon Tyne.

Based on the classic CGP style created by Richard Parsons.

Contents

Introduction to the Unit

An Introduction to Russia in the 19th Century 2
An Introduction to Marx 4

Section 1 — Challenges to the Romanovs, 1881-1905

Introduction to Section 1 5
Alexander III (1881-1894) 6
Economic Change (1881-1914) 8
Opposition to Tsarism 10
The 1905 Revolution 12

Section 2 — The Downfall of the Romanovs, 1906-1917

Introduction to Section 2 14
The Dumas (1906-1914) 15
Stolypin — Repression and Reform 16
Russia and the First World War 18
The February Revolution 1917 20

Section 3 — The Bolshevik Triumph of 1917

Introduction to Section 3 22
Dual Power 23
Opposition to the Provisional Government 24
The Provisional Government in Crisis 26

Section 4 — The Establishment of Bolshevik Power, 1917-1924

Introduction to Section 4 28
The Bolsheviks Take Control (1917-1918) 29
Civil War and Foreign Intervention (1918-1921) 32
Bolshevik Economic Policies (1917-1924) 35

Section 5 — Exam Skills

The Exam 38
The Mark Scheme 39
How to Structure Your Answer 40
How to Structure Paragraphs 41

Section 6 — Writing Your Answer

Sample Multi-Factor Question 42
How to Select the Right Information 43
How to Plan Your Answer 45
Worked Answer 46
Sample Single-Factor Question 50
How to Select the Right Information 51
How to Plan Your Answer 54
Worked Answer 55
Sample 'Why' Type Question 58
How to Select the Right Information 59
How to Plan Your Answer 62
Worked Answer 63

Index 66

An Introduction to Russia in the 19th Century

This page will introduce you to Russia. Don't be shy — you should get to know each other a bit better. I bet that by the end of the page you'll be firm friends.

Russia's **Population** was very **Diverse**

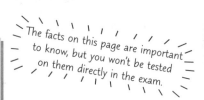
The facts on this page are important to know, but you won't be tested on them directly in the exam.

1) In the **19th century**, most of Russia's population were Russian, but there were **significant minorities** including:
   - Ukrainians
   - Georgians
   - Finns
   - Poles

2) The empire's population was **concentrated** in the **western** part of the country.

3) **Controlling** such a **diverse population** was **very difficult**.

The **Main Religion** in Russia was **Orthodox Christianity**

1) **Most Russians** were members of the **Russian Orthodox Church**.
2) The Church taught **complete obedience** to the **Tsar** and that to resist the Tsar was a **serious sin**.
3) There were many **Roman Catholics** in **Poland** and **Ukraine**.
4) A large **Muslim** population lived in the **east** of the **empire**.
5) **Several million Jews** lived in the **west** of **Russia**.

Russia was **Ruled** by the **Royal Family**

1) The **rulers** of **Russia** were the **Tsars**. Since **1613** the **Tsars** had **all** come from the **Romanov family**.
2) The Tsarist system was an **autocracy** (rule by one person).
3) The Tsar ruled by **decree**. His word was **law**.
4) Tsars claimed to rule by **divine right**, which meant they were only **answerable** to **God**.
5) The Tsar had **ministers** to **help govern** the country. In the countryside, **local nobility enforced** the Tsar's will.
6) Autocracy went **unchallenged** in Russia until the middle of the 19th century. But as Russia **modernised**, people wanted **more say** in how their country was **governed**.

Russia's **Economy** was **Based** on **Agriculture**

1) Unlike other European countries, Russia **hadn't** experienced an **agricultural** or **industrial revolution**.
2) The vast **majority** of the population were **peasants** who **farmed small plots** of **land**. Many of them **didn't** have **enough land** to grow more crops than those needed to **feed** their **families**.
3) Until 1861 there were **millions** of **serfs** who **weren't free**. They were effectively **owned** by the Tsar, the nobles or the Orthodox Church.
4) There **wasn't** enough **fertile land** for Russia's **massive population** of **peasants**.

Russia — a big old place...

Russia in the 19th century was huge and there was massive diversity across all four corners of the empire. Despite being so big, Russia wasn't strong economically or militarily and there was a lot that needed to be done to make it into a major European power.

An Introduction to Russia in the 19th Century

This page gives you background to the reigns Alexander III and Nicholas II. The starting date for the topic is 1881, so while you don't need to know anything before that for the exam, it'll help you understand what happened later.

Russia was **Developing Slowly**

1) Russia was an **agricultural** country. **80%** of the population worked on the **land**.

2) There was some **limited industrial development** in the **west**, around Moscow, St. Petersburg and the Baltic States.

3) Russia's population, however, grew rapidly, from approximately **68.5 million** in **1850** to **125 million** in **1897**.

4) Coal mining grew **rapidly** in the **Donbass region** in **Ukraine**.

The ever expanding Russian population.

Alexander II *made some* **Big Changes**

Russia suffered a **humiliating** defeat in the **Crimean War** (**1854-56**). This persuaded Alexander II (1855-81) to make some **major domestic reforms** which he hoped would **modernise** the country and the army.

1) Alexander's **most important** act was the **emancipation** (freeing) of the **serfs** in **1861**. **All** the **serfs** became **free peasants** and **Alexander** ensured **every peasant** was given a **small plot** of **land** to farm. They were also given other **freedoms**, like being allowed to **marry** without the land owner's consent.

2) To pay for this, the serfs were charged **redemption payments** over the next **49 years**.

3) Alexander reformed the **military**, **local government** and the **system** of **justice**. **Primary education** was expanded and **universities** were given more **freedom**.

Over 20 million serfs were emancipated in 1861.

Alexander II became known as the '**Tsar Liberator**' for freeing the serfs. However, his reforms, **especially** the university reforms, **encouraged** the development of **radical political groups**.

Radical groups became more **Militant**

1) The radical groups wanted Alexander's reforms to **go further**.

2) Some wanted Tsarist **autocracy** to be **replaced** with a **parliamentary** system like that in Britain.

3) The political views of **Karl Marx** (see page 4) and the anarchist **Michael Bakunin** became **popular** in Russia at this time.

4) In the **1870s**, radicals formed several **terrorist groups**. The most important was called the **People's Will**.

5) In **March 1881**, Alexander II was preparing to allow a Duma (a national parliament) to be elected, but he was **assassinated** in **St. Petersburg** by members of the **People's Will**.

> **Alexander II** and his son, **Alexander III**, created **counter-revolutionary organisations** to **suppress radicalism** and drive it underground. These became the secret police force known as the **Okhrana**. Alexander's successors set themselves **firmly against** any further **liberal reforms**.

Alexander II wanted to move Russia forward...

Alexander II's reforms were designed to modernise Russia so the humiliation of the Crimean War wouldn't be repeated. Despite this, Alexander didn't want to limit his own powers and he was assassinated by radicals who wanted him to do more. Unsurprisingly, Alexander's successors weren't keen to mess around with revolutionaries and used the Okhrana to suppress them.

An Introduction to Marx

If you're going to understand the rest of the book then it's really important to know about Karl Marx, and why his theories were so popular in this period.

Workers were Exploited by their employers

1) Russia, unlike most European nations at that time, was still a partly **feudal society** — the land was worked by **millions** of **serfs** who were **controlled** and **exploited** by their lords (almost like slaves). The **emancipation** of the **serfs** (see page 3) in Russia **didn't** suddenly make everything great. The **oppression** of the **peasants continued**.

2) In the **19th century**, **capitalists** were very **powerful**. They included factory owners whose aim was to make as much money as possible. This was often done by **exploiting** their workers.

3) Workers often worked **long hours**, in **unsafe conditions**, and lived in **squalid housing**.

4) Such poor working and living conditions caused **great unrest**. Marx's theories **appealed** to many **Russians** because they wanted to **overthrow** their **capitalist** leaders and create a more **equal society**.

Marx believed Class Struggle would Abolish Capitalism

Marx argued that the "history of all hitherto existing society is the history of class struggles." He believed society had **developed through history** and would **develop further** in **future**. Society would pass through **several phases** before people eventually became **equal**.

Karl Marx (1818-1883)

1) **Class struggle** would lead to the **abolition** of **feudalism**. The **emancipation** of the **serfs** was part of this process.

2) Industrialisation caused the **oppression** of the **workers**. Eventually they would **rise up** and **overthrow** their **capitalist** oppressors in a **revolution**.

3) Society would then move to a **new phase** — **socialism**. The state would be in charge of everything, and **all social classes** would be **abolished**.

4) Once **classes** had been abolished, **society** would **move** into its **final** and **permanent stage** — **communism**.

5) In a communist state **every person** would **work** for the **benefit of all**, so there would be **no need** for a **central government**.

Practice Questions

Q1 'It was difficult for the Tsars to promote unity in Russia.' Write a list of reasons to support this statement.

Q2 Why do you think Alexander II's two successors (Alexander III and Nicholas II) were opposed to making reforms in Russia?

Q3 Write a paragraph explaining why Marx's theories would appeal to many Russians.

Q4 In no more than 50 words explain how Marx believed society would develop towards communism.

Get your facts right, and you'll soon be getting top Marx...

It'd be silly to learn everything about Russia in the 19th century, but if you study these pages well enough, you'll be off on the right foot. It should be pretty useful in understanding the events that happened next — right... over... this... page...

Introduction to Section 1

This page will help you learn the key dates, key people and the historical vocab that you're going to need to remember from Section 1. So use this page wisely young padawan, and learn this stuff so that you can really impress the examiner.

Here's a **Quick Summary** of **Section One**

This section deals with the **reign** of **Alexander III** (1881-1894) and the **early years** of **Nicholas II's reign** (1894-1917). **Three big things** were going on at the time:

1. Repression

- 1881-1905 was a period of **political repression**.
- The Tsars **suppressed** groups, such as the **Socialist Revolutionaries** and the **Social Democrats**, who were **demanding reform**.

2. Industrialisation

- This period also saw **major economic changes** as Russia underwent **rapid industrialisation**.
- However, **modernisation wasn't** very **popular** with ordinary people.

3. 1905 Revolution

- This period ends with the **1905 Revolution** — an **attack** on **Tsarism**.
- The Revolution **ended** when Nicholas II **promised concessions** in the **October Manifesto**.

Learn the **Key Dates** of the **Romanov Troubles**

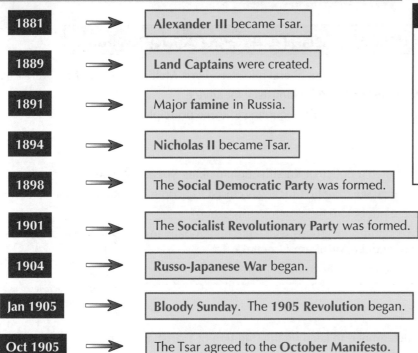

1881 ⟹	**Alexander III** became Tsar.
1889 ⟹	**Land Captains** were created.
1891 ⟹	Major **famine** in Russia.
1894 ⟹	**Nicholas II** became Tsar.
1898 ⟹	The **Social Democratic Party** was formed.
1901 ⟹	The **Socialist Revolutionary Party** was formed.
1904 ⟹	**Russo-Japanese War** began.
Jan 1905 ⟹	**Bloody Sunday**. The **1905 Revolution** began.
Oct 1905 ⟹	The Tsar agreed to the **October Manifesto**.

Important People in this Period:

- **Nikolai Bunge** — Finance Minister, 1881-1887.
- **Ivan Vyshnegradsky** — Finance Minister, 1887-1892.
- **Sergei Witte** — Finance Minister, 1892-1903.
- **Constantine Pobedonostsev** — Alexander III and Nicholas II's tutor.

The Tsar's favourite method of control.

Make sure you know what these **Historical Terms** mean

- **Tsarism** — A form of government run by a Tsar.
- **Autocracy** — One person rules with absolute power.
- **Okhrana** — The Russian Secret Police.
- **Marxism** — A set of theories put forward by Marx.

- **Constitutional government** — A government based on a set of agreed rules.
- **Redemption payments** — Money owed to the government by the peasants for their land.
- **Duma** — The Russian parliament.

Alexander III (1881-1894)

A lot of people forget about this stuff and launch straight in to learning about the First World War instead. Don't ignore these pages — they're quite interesting really. And there's the added bonus that two of the Tsars have the same name.

Alexander II believed in Autocracy (one person having Absolute Power)

1) **Tsar Alexander II** (reigned 1855-81) made **major changes** during the first ten years of his rule — e.g. the **emancipation** (freeing) of the **serfs** in **1861** (see page 3).

2) During his later years he went back to the more **traditional** Tsarist system of **autocracy**.

3) Alexander II had just agreed to the creation of a new **partly elected national assembly** to advise him, when in March 1881 he was **assassinated** in St. Petersburg by members of the **People's Will**.

Alexander III was even more Repressive

Alexander III **didn't** attempt any **reform** at all. He was **reactionary** (against reform) and **inflexible**. For example:

> 1) After Alexander II was assassinated, Alexander III issued the Temporary Regulations. They gave provincial governors and officials the power to imprison people without trial, ban public meetings and exile thousands of offenders to Siberia.
>
> 2) The Okhrana (secret police) restricted the press and monitored revolutionary and socialist groups.

Alexander III was heavily influenced by his Tutor — Pobedonostsev

1) After Alexander II's assassination the government's more **liberal** ministers, **Loris-Melikov** and **Ignatiev**, were **sacked**.

2) The new Tsar relied on his former tutor **Constantine Pobedonostsev** for **advice**.

3) Pobedonostsev believed that it was the Tsar's duty to rule according to **three principles**:

(1) Nationality

- Alexander III and Pobedonostsev promoted a policy of **Russification** (making Russia **more Russian**).
- In **1885** Russian became the **official language**. **Public office** was **closed** to people who couldn't speak it fluently.
- The rights of the Russian **majority** were put before those of minority groups.
- Alexander III **didn't distinguish** between minority groups who were traditionally **loyal** to Tsarism (e.g. Finns), and groups who **opposed** it (e.g. Poles and the Muslims of Central Asia).
- This **increased opposition** to Tsarism from many different sections of society.

> Russia was a huge empire with millions of people of different cultures. Russification was introduced as a method of controlling them.

(2) Autocracy

- Alexander III declared that he was determined to **keep up** the **tradition** of **Tsarist autocracy**.
- In 1889 **elected** Justices of the Peace were replaced by the **Land Captains** — **aristocrats** appointed by the **Tsar**.
- Land Captains could **overrule** the zemstva (local council) and **charge peasant farmers** with minor offences.
- Peasants felt that the Land Captains treated them as **badly** as they had been during the years of **serfdom**.
- In 1890 the Tsar **restricted** the **right to vote** for the zemstva in the countryside, and in 1892 the right to vote for the **dumas** in the towns was restricted in a similar way. This gave the landed gentry even more power.

(3) Orthodoxy

- The rights and privileges of the **Russian Orthodox Church** were championed above those of other beliefs.
- **Primary schools** came under **Church control**.

Alexander III (1881-1894)

Alexander III's rule was a bit of a shock to the Russian people, especially in contrast to the rule of his fairly liberal father. Many people suffered under his rule, but none more so than the Jews...

Jews Suffered *the most under Russification*

Anti-Semitism was **common** in **Russia** and the **Jews** were made into a **target** by Tsar **Alexander III**.

Loss of rights	• Jewish people **weren't allowed** to become **doctors** or **lawyers**. • **Very few** were admitted to **universities**.

Violence	• Organised violent attacks called **pogroms** had been carried out on Jewish communities in Russia for a long time. • They **increased** under Russification because they were **encouraged** by the government. • There were over **200 pogroms** during Alexander III's reign.

The **Jews responded** *in two important ways*

1) Many Jews **left the country** and resettled in Western Europe and the USA.
2) Others formed a **radical organisation** called the **Bund**, which worked with the opposition parties in the years before 1917.

© Illustrated London News Ltd/Mary Evans

Alexander III (1845-1894)

Summary of **Alexander III's Reign**

1) He provided **firm leadership** and a **clear direction** for the government.
2) He brought back **strong autocratic power**, underpinned by the **Church**, the **aristocracy** and the **army**.
3) He still had **opposition**, but it had been **weakened** and **driven underground**.
4) However, he found it **difficult** to tackle the **problems** emerging in his rapidly **industrialising** country.
5) He left a **legacy** of **repression** and **autocracy**, which Nicholas II continued.

Practice Questions

Q1 Write a paragraph defending Alexander III's policies.

Q2 Which policies do you find difficult to defend? Explain your answer.

Q3 Summarise Alexander III's system of government in no more than 25 words.

Q4 'Alexander III was an unpopular yet effective ruler.' To what extent do you agree with this statement?

Glossary

The dumas — elected town councils. (The national elected assembly would be known as the Duma.)

Don't get the two Alexanders confused...

You don't need to know lots about Alexander II's reign — this topic starts with his assassination in 1881, but it's helpful to know a bit of background information. Alexander III is the man you need to look out for — his rule was very eventful.

Economic Change (1881-1914)

Russia went through lots of economic changes as it moved from an agriculture-based economy to an industrial one. But not all the reforms were successful, and some of them caused resentment...

In *1881* the *Economy* was still based on *Agriculture*

The **emancipation** of the **serfs** (1861) **didn't change** the Russian economy much over the next 20 years.

1) It carried on being **dependent** on **agricultural** production, especially **grain**.
2) **Very few** Russians **worked** in **industry** — over **80%** of the population lived in the **countryside**.
3) Russian cities were **small** by European standards. Moscow and St. Petersburg had populations of **under a million**.

The *Tsars Modernised* Russia through *Industrialisation*

1) Russia's **population** was **growing rapidly**. It almost doubled between **1881** and **1914**. This led to **overpopulation** of the countryside and put **pressure** on **landholdings**.
2) Russia wanted to **maintain** its status as a **great power**. This meant that Russia had to **industrialise** to **compete** with other great powers like **Germany** and **Britain**.
3) So **Alexander III** and **Nicholas II** decided to take **direct action** to **force** industrialisation.

Industrialisation was carried out by *Three Key Players*

Russia's economic reform was undertaken by **three** Finance Ministers:

1 *Nikolai Bunge (1881-1887)*

- Bunge created the **Peasants' Land Bank** which was intended to **encourage peasants** to **expand** their **landholdings**.

However, the Peasants' Land Bank was **too small** to be **effective**.

Thanks Pheasants' Loan Bank! With the £3000 I borrowed I was able to start up my own wheat field.

2 *Ivan Vyshnegradsky (1887-1892)*

- To raise money for industrialisation, Vyshnegradsky **encouraged foreign investment** and **increased taxes**.
- **Foreigners** were enticed to invest with **incentives**. This helped the **expansion** of the **small railway network**, and the growth of **heavy industry** in **Ukraine** and **oil production** in **Baku**.
- Domestic industries (e.g. oil and coal) were **protected** with **high tariffs** to boost consumer demand.

But, Vyshnegradsky **exported** a lot of **grain** to **finance** his policies. This continued **despite** a **major famine** at home in 1891. He was **sacked** in 1892.

3 *Sergei Witte (1892-1903)*

- Witte was the **most important** Finance Minister of this period.
- Industrial growth in other countries had been driven by a **large middle class** — which **didn't exist** in Russia at this time.
- In the **absence** of a large middle class, **Witte** developed a policy of **state intervention** in the Russian economy.

Economic Change (1881-1914)

Witte Focused on the Railways and Foreign Investment

Witte's policies aimed at **improving the Russian economy** by focusing on two key areas.

Railways	• The **Trans-Siberian Railway** was started in **1891**. The railway **opened up** the eastern empire and **advanced** the growth of **new towns** and **cities**. • A network of railways was planned for western Russia to **link new industrial centres**. • A new railway **linked** the **oil refineries** of **Baku** to the Black Sea port of **Batum**. • This helped to **stimulate the growth** of the **iron** and **coal industries**.
Foreign Investment	• In **1897** Witte put the **rouble** on the **gold standard** — guaranteeing the currency's value. • This encouraged western countries — especially **France** and **Belgium** — to **invest heavily** in Russian industry. • Foreign investment **increased** from **roughly 200 million rubles** in **1890** to approximately **900 million rubles** in **1900**.

There were Pros and Cons to Witte's Policies

Pros	1) Heavy industry saw **massive increases** in production, especially of **coal** and **iron**. 2) Output from the **Baku** oil refineries **increased tenfold** between **1883** and **1900**. 3) The **economy grew** rapidly by an estimated **8% a year** in the **1890s**. 4) Growth briefly stalled for a few years — but from **1906** to **1914** the **economy grew** by **6%** a year.
Cons	1) The **Trans-Siberian Railway** was built to **encourage** migration to areas where workers were needed. But by 1914, it was only **partially finished** and it **didn't increase** migration by very much. 2) Witte **raised taxes** in order to provide money for **industrial developments**. 3) These taxes **squeezed the peasants**, making them less likely to spend on consumer goods. 4) The government ran up **enormous debts**. 5) **State control** of **industry** meant that the **middle class** grew **slowly** in the years before **1914**. 6) Witte **didn't improve** the state of the **agriculture industry** — even though **taxes on the peasants** accounted for over **80%** of the **government's income**.

Practice Questions

Q1 Write a paragraph explaining why the Tsars decided to industrialise Russia.

Q2 Look at the pros and cons of Witte's policies. Imagine you are Sergei Witte — try to explain why you think that the benefits your policies have created for Russia outweigh the negatives.

Glossary

Gold Standard — where a unit of a country's currency is worth a fixed weight of gold.

Peasants' Land Bank — organisation which provided peasants with cheap loans to purchase land.

So many finance ministers — so little time...

Now there's a sentence I never thought I'd write. Witte is the one to focus on though — the other two didn't do particularly well. Make sure you're keeping track of all these complicated Russian names. If you confuse the three finance ministers it will be pretty costly in the exam. It might be helpful to make a list of all the important names — that should help you learn the spelling too...

Opposition to Tsarism

You need to know how economic reform affected everyday life in Russia. Generally the Russian people were unhappy with the changes the government made, making the Tsar less popular than overcooked sprouts at Christmas...

Industrialisation was Good for Russia's Economy... but Bad for Russians

1) The economic reforms carried out in this period **strengthened** the Russian economy. In **1881** Russia had the world's **11th** largest economy. By **1914** it had the world's **fifth** largest. But...

2) Industrialisation **didn't** make for a happy society. The **gap** between rich and poor **increased** and society became **divided** between the **countryside** and the **town**.

Peasants

1) Most peasants were still paying the **redemption payments** imposed in return for the land they were given when they became free.

2) The peasants now farmed **smaller landholdings** than they'd had before emancipation. The **nobles** had **kept the best land** for themselves — leaving the peasants with **poor soil**.

3) Farming practices **hadn't evolved** much since the Middle Ages — e.g. **old-fashioned crop rotation** (where each year some fields are not sown with crops) was still common.

4) **Peasants couldn't leave** their village without the **permission** of the **mir** (the whole community). So they still **weren't** really **free**.

5) The **gap** between **rich** and **poor** peasants grew. **Richer** peasants (**kulaks**) **gained more land** and **ran local businesses**.

6) Many peasants **migrated** to the towns to earn **extra money** when they **weren't needed** for **sowing** and **harvesting**.

Urban Workers

1) Many town workers earned **barely enough** to survive from one week to the next.

2) Factory hours were **not regulated** by the state until Witte introduced an **11½ hour working day** in **1897**. However, this law was **often ignored**.

3) Factories were meant to be regularly inspected, but **safety rules** usually **weren't followed**.

4) The **rapid growth** of towns meant that workers lived in **overcrowded** and **insanitary tenements**.

5) **Health** and **education** services were **poor**, creating more social inequality.

6) **Life expectancy** was **under 30 years**.

This Increased Social Unrest

In the Countryside

1) **Unrest** amongst the peasants **grew** as their needs were put **after** the need to industrialise.

2) Peasants **resented** the **higher taxes** and were **bitter** about the **lack of government support** during famines.

In the Towns

1) **Industrial labourers** suffered the most under Witte's industrialisation of Russia.

2) They **weren't allowed** to form **trade unions** and there were **no legal political parties** to represent their needs.

3) Although **town dwellers** only accounted for **20%** of the population, they became an **increasingly radical force**.

Middle-Class Reformists formed the Liberals

Nicholas II said that a constitutional government was 'a senseless dream'.

1) The economic reforms led to the growth of a **new, educated middle class**. Many of the **politically active** members of this class became **liberals**.

2) They **weren't completely opposed** to Tsarism, but they wanted the **autocracy** of the Tsars to be replaced with a **constitutional government**.

3) In **1903** liberals formed the **League of Liberation**, which wanted a **shorter working day**, **more land** for the peasants, and an **elected parliament**.

- The middle class gained **political experience** through the zemstva (local councils).
- They organised **health** and **education** services and built **roads** and **bridges**.
- They provided **food** for starving peasants during **famines**, as government support was **inadequate**.

Opposition to Tsarism

The Socialist Revolutionaries were Revolutionary Socialists

1) The **Socialist Revolutionaries** (SRs) grew out of earlier groups known as the **Populists**. They believed that **revolution** would begin in the **countryside**. They tried unsuccessfully to **convert peasants** into **revolutionaries**.

2) In **1901** Populist groups **joined** to form the **Socialist Revolutionary Party** — a party for both **urban labourers** and **peasants**. They aimed to:

- **Redistribute land** to the peasants.
- **Improve living** and **working conditions** in towns.
- **Overthrow Tsarism** by **force**.

3) The **SRs** used **terrorism** to advance their **political aims**. Between **1901** and **1905** SR terrorists **assassinated** several **leading politicians**, including the **Tsar's uncle**, who was **Governor** of **Moscow**.

The Social Democrats were Marxists

1) The **Social Democrats** (SDs) followed the political beliefs of **Karl Marx** (see page 4).

2) In **1898** they brought together a number of Russian Marxist groups to form the **Russian Social Democratic Workers' Party**. This included members who would later split off to become the **Bolsheviks**, a group who supported Lenin and his ideas, and the **Mensheviks**, a group who preferred a less disciplined, more democratic form of communism.

- The **Okhrana** (the **Secret Police**) kept a close eye on the **SDs**. The Tsars **feared** Marxism because of its **revolutionary principles**.
- In **1899** several leading members were **arrested**, including **Vladimir Ulyanov**, who was **exiled** to central Russia.
- While in exile **Ulyanov** adopted a new surname taken from the **River Lena** — his name became **Vladimir Lenin**.

The Opposition Parties Didn't get very Far

1) Although **many political** parties emerged in Russia in the early 20th century, they were all **too small** and **ineffective** to achieve their **aims**.

2) There were also **major divisions** between the parties, which made them **less effective** at opposing the government.

3) The political parties faced **constant harassment** and **violence** from the Okhrana.

Practice Questions

Q1 Give some examples of why the peasants were unhappy.

Q2 Give some examples of why the urban workers were unhappy.

Q3 What were the aims of the Socialist Revolutionaries?

Q4 Which party did the Bolsheviks and the Mensheviks split from?

Exam Question

Q1 To what extent was the industrialisation of Russia beneficial to the Russian people?   [30 marks]

The Tsar managed to stopposition the opposition...

Make sure you mention in your essays that economic reforms made the government unpopular with the majority of Russians. Economic reform sounds good, but don't let the positive name throw you — it made a lot of people's lives worse.

The 1905 Revolution

The 1905 Revolution was a major crisis for the government and came as a result of both long- and short-term causes. The Russian people had been unhappy for years, but it was the events of Bloody Sunday that triggered major unrest.

The 1905 Revolution had Long- and Short-term Causes

Long-term Causes

- The rapidly growing towns and cities didn't have good **sanitation** or **water supplies**.
- There were **huge pressures** on **food supplies** and **famine** was **common**.
- **High taxes** and **redemption payments** left the peasants very poor and desperate for more land.
- Political parties were **growing**, despite efforts by the Okhrana to **suppress** them.
- Nicholas II remained committed to **autocracy**.

Long-term causes provide the conditions for an event to take place. Short-term causes explain why the event took place at a particular time. They're both important.

Short-term Causes

- In **1904** Russia and **Japan** were at war. Russia suffered a number of **humiliating** defeats — especially **Port Arthur** in **January 1905**.
- **Bloody Sunday** shocked many Russians and **badly damaged** the Tsar's **authority** and **prestige**.

Bloody Sunday

1) On **Sunday 9th January 1905 Father Gapon**, an Orthodox priest, led a **peaceful** march to the **Winter Palace** in **St. Petersburg** to present a **petition** to the Tsar. **150 000** workers attended.
2) **Gapon** petitioned for:
   - An **end** to the **war** with Japan.
   - **Fair wages** and an **eight-hour** working day.
   - The election of a **national** parliament.
3) **Soldiers** guarding the palace **opened fire**, **killing hundreds** of **unarmed** people.

Bloody Sunday triggered the 1905 Revolution

1) A **month** after **Bloody Sunday**, around **half a million** workers went on **strike** in **protest** at the massacre. By the end of the year this had risen to **2.7 million**.

2) The strikes **affected** the **railways**, so food couldn't be delivered to the towns and cities.

3) The **peasants** took this **opportunity** to revolt — **illegally** taking land from the landowners.

- Army **morale** was **dented** by the **loss** of the **Russian Baltic** fleet at the **Battle** of **Tsushima** (against Japan).
- In **June 1905** the crew of the **Battleship Potemkin** mutinied. They **killed** their **officers** and **bombarded** the port of **Odessa**.

4) In **July 1905** the **All-Russian Peasants' Union** met in **Moscow**, but **struggled** to **organise** the peasants at a **national level**. They had **similar aims** to the **Socialist Revolutionaries**.

5) **National minorities** engaged in **widespread protests**. Most of these took place in the **western** part of the empire, but there were also **serious disturbances** in **Armenia**.

6) In **St. Petersburg** a council (**Soviet**) was elected by **factory workers**. The **St. Petersburg Soviet** organised **strikes** and **demonstrations**. The Soviet was **dominated** by the **Mensheviks**, including **Leon Trotsky**.

The 1905 Revolution

Nicholas II had to make Concessions to Keep Control

1) In **August**, Nicholas announced the formation of an elected **Duma** (parliament). But it had **no power** to pass laws, only to advise the Tsar.

2) This **pleased no one**. In October **strikes** brought the country to a **standstill**.

3) **Witte** proposed **new concessions**, which the Tsar reluctantly agreed to. On **17th October**, Nicholas published the **October Manifesto**.

Nicholas wanted to resort to a military dictatorship to suppress the unrest. But his ministers persuaded him against this.

The October Manifesto promised...

- Freedom of **speech**, **religion** and a **free press**.
- An **elected Duma** which had **actual authority**. Laws issued by the **Tsar needed** the **approval** of the Duma.
- In **November** a **second manifesto** was published. It promised to **improve** the **Peasants' Land Bank** and to **abolish redemption payments** within a year.

4) The October Manifesto **worked** and the **strikes** were **called off**.

5) **Spontaneous** demonstrations in **favour** of the Tsar were held in St. Petersburg.

6) The **St. Petersburg Soviet** was dissolved.

7) A **December** uprising in **Moscow**, led by **Bolsheviks**, was easily **crushed**.

1905 was a Fresh Start for Nicholas II

You could argue that what happened in 1905 actually **strengthened** Nicholas's position:

1) The **army** and the **police** remained **loyal** to the government.

2) The political parties were taken by **surprise** and **didn't coordinate** an effective opposition to the Tsar.

3) Many revolutionary leaders were in **exile** and couldn't capitalise on the unrest.

The October Manifesto split the opposition to Tsarism

- The Bolsheviks, Mensheviks and the Socialist Revolutionaries **remained hostile** to the Tsar.
- The Liberals **welcomed** the Manifesto — it was a **milestone** toward the **reform** they wanted.
- **Some** Liberals wanted a **full written constitution** and became known as **Constitutional Democrats** (better known as the **Kadets**).
- One group felt the October Manifesto was **final** — they were known as '**Octobrists**'.

Practice Questions

Q1 Write a paragraph on whether the events of 1905 strengthened or weakened Tsarism.

Q2 Why did Tsar Nicholas II agree to the October Manifesto?

Exam Question

Q1 A revolution is an attempt to overthrow the government.
To what extent were the events of 1905 a 'revolution'?

[30 marks]

Bloody Sunday — not just a U2 song...

With a little more organisation and planning it could have all been so different — the Tsar came pretty close to being overthrown by anti-Tsarists trying to capitalise on Russia's unrest, but he managed to survive with some clever political manoeuvring.

Introduction to Section 2

Here's another amazing, super awesome page dedicated to key dates, key people and the historical vocab that will help you ace your exam. Have fun learning it all — you'd be daft not to...

Here's a **Quick Summary** of **Section Two**

This section deals with the **last years** of Nicholas II's reign and the **end** of **Tsarism** in Russia. Here's what you should know:

- The **Dumas** changed the way the country was run... a **bit.**
- Prime Minister **Peter Stolypin** introduced important **reforms** in the **agricultural system.**
- In **1914**, Russia joined the **First World War** and fought against **Germany** and **Austria-Hungary.**
- **Long-term** and **short-term** pressures on Tsarism led to the **1917 February Revolution** which **ended 300 years** of the **Romanov** dynasty's **rule.**

Learn the **Key Dates** of the **Romanov Troubles**

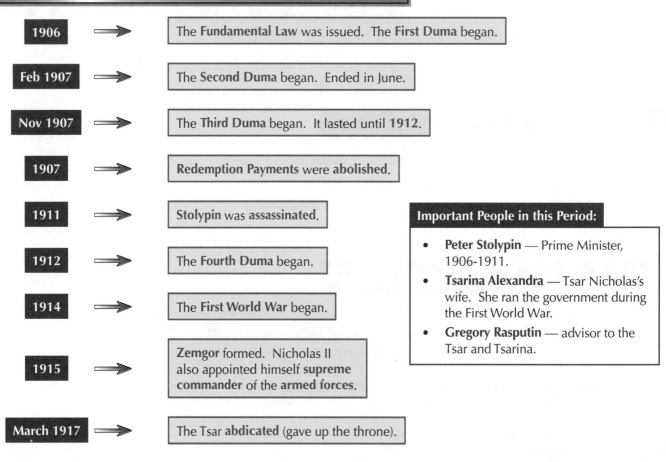

1906	⟹	The **Fundamental Law** was issued. The **First Duma** began.
Feb 1907	⟹	The **Second Duma** began. Ended in June.
Nov 1907	⟹	The **Third Duma** began. It lasted until **1912**.
1907	⟹	**Redemption Payments** were **abolished.**
1911	⟹	**Stolypin** was **assassinated.**
1912	⟹	The **Fourth Duma** began.
1914	⟹	The **First World War** began.
1915	⟹	**Zemgor** formed. Nicholas II also appointed himself **supreme commander** of the **armed forces.**
March 1917	⟹	The Tsar **abdicated** (gave up the throne).

Important People in this Period:

- **Peter Stolypin** — Prime Minister, 1906-1911.
- **Tsarina Alexandra** — Tsar Nicholas's wife. She ran the government during the First World War.
- **Gregory Rasputin** — advisor to the Tsar and Tsarina.

Make sure you know what these **Historical Terms** mean

- **Octobrists** — A party that supported the constitutional changes of the October Manifesto.
- **Bolsheviks** — A radical party that wanted a revolution.
- **Mensheviks** — A less radical party that wanted a revolution.
- **Kadets** — A party that wanted a new constitution to be worked out by an elected assembly.

- **Provisional Government** — Temporary government that took over after the Tsar abdicated.
- **Zemgor** — An organisation that helped the government in the First World War.

The Dumas (1906-1914)

The Duma was introduced to pacify opposition. There were four in all — some were more successful than others.

Nicholas II introduced the Fundamental Law

From October 1905 **stability** had largely been restored. In **March 1906** Nicholas issued the **Fundamental Law of the Russian Empire** which broke some of the promises he made in the October Manifesto and **reasserted** his authority:

1) The Tsar had **supreme autocratic power**.
2) The Tsar could govern by **issuing decrees** (Article 87).
3) The **Council of State** would be set up — a **parliamentary body** made up of **Tsarist sympathisers**.
4) Laws proposed by the **Duma** had to be approved by the **Council of State** and the **Tsar** — **reform** seemed **unlikely**.
5) Government ministers were **appointed by the Tsar** and only had to answer to him — not the Duma.

The First Duma (April to June 1906) was made up of Four Main Parties

Trudoviks
Represented the **peasants** and the **workers**.

Octobrists
Moderate — **loyal to the Tsar**.

Progressives
New party made up of **businessmen**.

Kadets
Supported by **intellectuals** and **professionals**.

Some radical left-wing parties, e.g. the Bolsheviks, boycotted the elections to the First Duma.

These parties made **radical demands**:

- **All adult males** should have the **vote**.
- Major **land reforms** should be introduced to **benefit** the **peasants**.
- **Political prisoners** should be **released**.
- **Ministers** should be **answerable** to the **Duma**.

1) Nicholas **refused** their demands. After 72 days of stalemate he **dissolved** the Duma.
2) Deputies gathered in Vyborg (Finland) and **appealed** to the Russian people to **protest** the dissolution of the Duma.
3) Nicholas responded by **arresting** the deputies and **banning** them from standing for election in the future.

There were Three more Dumas between 1907 and 1917

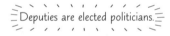
Deputies are elected politicians.

	Parties present	Summary
Second Duma Feb 1907 - June 1907	• The number of Kadet deputies **dropped**. • Seats were **gained by the Socialist Revolutionaries, the Bolsheviks** and the **Mensheviks**.	• Passed important **land reform** proposed by **Stolypin**. • Existed in a state of almost constant **uproar**. • Lasted for just **four months**.
Third Duma Nov 1907 - June 1912	• The **electoral system** was revised — **peasants lost the vote**. This meant that the deputies were all fairly **conservative**. • The **Octobrists** were the **largest party** present.	• More **right-wing**, so prepared to **work with** the **government** rather than **challenge** it. • Most proposals from the government were **passed** e.g. further **land reforms** presented by Stolypin and a fairly progressive system of **insurance** for **factory workers**. • Lasted for **over four years**.
Fourth Duma Nov 1912 - Feb 1917	• Dominated by the **Octobrists** and other **right-wing** parties.	• Worked with the government until the outbreak of **war** in August 1914, but its significance **changed** dramatically as the war **progressed** (see page 19).

The Third and Fourth Dumas made some Progress

1) The hated system of **Land Captains** was replaced by the **Justices of the Peace** (elected officials who judged minor court cases).
2) There was a massive **increase** in **educational provision** for students of all ages.
3) **Political parties** which had been **attacked** by the Tsars and the Okhrana were now **legal**.
4) The debates which took place in the Dumas were widely **reported** and **discussed** in the **press**.
5) Nicholas II appeared to **change** his **attitude** towards the Dumas. In 1906 he wrote that he **spat** on the idea of a **constitution**, but six years later he wrote 'The Duma started **too fast**. Now it is **slower**, but **better**, and more **lasting**.'

Stolypin — Repression and Reform

Many Russians thought that Stolypin and his land reforms were the best hope for reforming and sustaining Tsarism, but they never seemed to quite get going. On top of this, his harsh methods of keeping control were very unpopular.

Stolypin had a Ruthless Attitude to Unrest

1) Stolypin was a **governor**. He used the **police** and the **army** to suppress unrest and keep a **firm grip** on his people.

2) In **1906** Nicholas appointed Stolypin as **Prime Minister**. By then most **revolutionary activity** had been put down, but there were still disturbances in the country, and **political assassinations** were happening more often.

3) Stolypin introduced a **new court system** where offenders were **rapidly tried** and **sentenced**. Thousands of rebels were tried, hundreds were **executed** and many were sentenced to **hard labour** or **exile**.

4) His strong measures were effective. By **1908** order had been **restored**, but Stolypin had made Tsarism even more **unpopular**.

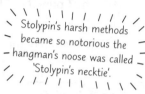
Stolypin's harsh methods became so notorious the hangman's noose was called 'Stolypin's necktie'.

The Russian Agricultural System was Inefficient

1) **Serfdom** had been **abolished** but peasants remained under the **control** of the mir (the community).

2) Each family had their share of land in **different fields** rather than working a single, more efficient landholding, and **farming techniques** were **outdated**.

The Consequences of the Problems with Russian Farming

- **Yields** were **low** compared with other European countries.
- **Famines** were **widespread** and **frequent**.
- Most peasants **couldn't** make a **profit**.
- The only peasants who were doing well were the **kulaks** (richer peasants), who were a **minority**.

Stolypin proposed Agricultural Reforms

Stolypin had **four main aims** in resolving the **agricultural problems**:

1) Increase the **prosperity** of peasants to develop a class of **well-off** agricultural workers.
2) Increase **crop yields**.
3) Have **fewer famines**.
4) Make the peasants **more content** and less likely to **rebel** against autocracy.

He proposed a series of **reforms**:

Land reforms

1) In **1906** the Tsar decreed that each peasant had an **unconditional right** to **land**.
2) They could **demand** their own **landholding** and farm it **without interference** from the **mir**.
3) Stolypin brought in **agricultural education** to train peasants in more advanced farming techniques in an attempt to **increase yields**.
4) He also sold vast areas of **Crown land** to the Peasant Land Bank for **resale** to the peasants, to increase the land **available** for farming.

Stolypin — Repression and Reform

Emigration to Siberia

1) Certain rural areas were **overcrowded**. Stolypin encouraged **migration** to Siberia where land was less densely populated, to try to **increase production**.
2) The completion of the **Trans-Siberian Railway** helped migrants move to Siberia.
3) Stolypin offered **incentives** to peasants who wanted to settle in the eastern regions of Russia, e.g. **cheap land** and some **tax exemptions**.
4) Around **3 million** peasants **relocated** to Siberia between **1908** and **1913**.

Other reforms

1) **Redemption payments** finally ended in **1907**.
2) **Internal passports** were abolished, so people had more **freedom**.
3) The unpopular **Land Captains** were replaced with elected **Justices of the Peace**.

"I'll boldly go where no land captain has gone before... the sea!"

The **Results** of **Stolypin's Reforms** were **Patchy...**

1) In reality few peasants could **afford** to **separate** from the mir and set up their own landholdings — only **25%** had done so by **1914**.
2) Stolypin hadn't addressed the problem that there was still **millions of hectares** owned by the **Tsar** and the **nobility**.
3) There was little change in **farming techniques**...
4) ... and not much increase in **farming output**.

... but it could be **Argued** that they **Weren't Given Enough Time**

- Stolypin knew that his **agricultural reforms** would need to be **developed** and **established** over many years.
- But he was **assassinated** in **1911**.
- Then **war** broke out in **1914**, meaning that the **long-term effects** of his reforms were **never realised**.

Practice Questions

Q1 Make a list of Stolypin's reforms. Write down one reason why he implemented each reform.

Q2 'Stolypin's assassination in 1911 was a disaster for Russia.'
How far do you agree with this statement?

Q3 Briefly assess whether Stolypin's reforms were a success or a failure.

Q4 Write down two reasons why Stolypin might have been:
   a) Popular with the Russian people.
   b) Unpopular with the Russian people.
   c) Popular with the Tsar
   d) Unpopular with the Tsar.

Stolypin — not the most caring of agricultural reformers...

If you're set a question on the economy in the years 1881-1914, make sure you write about Stolypin's land reforms. Even though they weren't entirely successful, they still had a big impact on the economy.

Russia and the First World War

*During the First World War Russia was fighting external enemies and trying to deal with internal problems too.
Although the war intensified these problems, it's important to remember that many of them already existed before 1914.*

The **War Highlighted Weaknesses** in **Russia's Government** and **Society**

1) Early in August **1914**, Germany and Austria-Hungary **declared war** on Russia.
2) To **outsiders**, Russia looked like a force to be reckoned with, but **internally**
its **military**, **society** and **government** were **falling apart**.
3) By **1917**, the **February Revolution** had toppled the Tsar's government.
4) The war highlighted **weaknesses** in Russia's **government** and **society**, which
contributed to the **downfall** of the Tsar. These were:

1) Armed Forces

1) **Millions** of men were conscripted into **large armies** known as the '**Russian steamroller'**.
2) Initial enthusiasm for the war was **shattered** by two early **defeats** at **Tannenberg** and the
Masurian Lakes in **1914**.
3) Conditions were **poor**. There were **insufficient food supplies** and a **lack** of **rifles** and **ammunition**.
4) Military **hospitals** were often **filthy** and had **insufficient medical supplies** — even bandages were
in short supply.
5) The **military command structure** was **inefficient**. Officers were chosen because of their **social
position** rather than their **military abilities**.
6) By **1916** the armed forces were **demoralised** and **undisciplined**. **Desertions** were common —
even during the successful Brusilov Offensive over **50 000** soldiers deserted from the army.

2) Transport

1) The **railway system** transported **troops** and **military equipment** — the needs of the army took **priority**.
2) The railways were **overloaded** in **peacetime** and by **1916** the system had **virtually collapsed**.
3) Armaments **factories** were producing plenty of **supplies** but the state of the railways meant they
couldn't be delivered. Not enough **food** was getting through. Lines were **blocked** by engine failures
and **grain** was left to **rot** in the sidings.
4) In **1916** food shortages were **widespread** and many people in towns were left **starving**.

3) The Economy

1) In **1914** the government abandoned the **gold standard**, which linked the value
of the rouble to Russia's gold reserves. This left the government free to **print** as
many **bank notes** as they wanted.
2) This policy led to **inflation** — wages could not keep up with **rapidly rising prices**.
3) By **1916** peasants realised that because of inflation it wasn't worth selling their
grain. So they started **hoarding** it — hoping for better times and **fairer prices**.
4) Russia's main ports for exporting goods were **blockaded**, which added to the
government's **economic difficulties**.

Russia and the First World War

(4) Nicholas and Alexandra

In 1914, St. Petersburg was renamed to the more Russian Petrograd.

1) In September **1915** Nicholas II appointed himself **Commander-in-Chief** of the armed forces. He was **away** from Petrograd for long periods of time.

2) Nicholas appointed his wife Alexandra to **supervise** the **government** in his place. Because she was **German**, it was rumoured that she was passing **military secrets** to her German relatives (even though she wasn't).

3) Alexandra constantly **changed ministers**, causing **instability** in the government.

© Mary Evans Picture Library

Gregory Rasputin (1869-1916)

Gregory Rasputin

- Alexandra was strongly **influenced** by Rasputin, a mystic who it seemed could **relieve** her son's **haemophilia**. She relied heavily on his advice and was **accused** of having an **affair** with him.

- The aristocracy and officials felt **threatened** by Rasputin's **importance** at court and his **power** over the royal family.

- He was **murdered** by aristocrats in December **1916**, but the **damage** he had caused couldn't be undone.

(5) Political Opposition

1) In **1914** most political parties **supported** the war effort and the Duma was **suspended**.

2) In **1915 failures** in the war forced Nicholas to **recall** the Duma.

3) The recalled Duma repeated the demands of the First Duma — a government which had **national support** and which would be **answerable** to the Duma.

4) Nicholas **rejected** this proposal and the Duma parties **united** to form the **Progressive Bloc** which continued to press for **changes** in the running of the war.

5) In **1915 Zemgor** was formed to **help** with the **war effort**. It provided **supplies** for **hospitals** and helped to organise smaller **industries** in towns and villages.

6) Nicholas was **suspicious** of Zemgor and **refused** to work with it.

Practice Questions

Q1 Summarise the five weaknesses of Russia's government and society in no more than 50 words each.

Q2 Which factor do you think was the most important in making the Tsar more unpopular? Give reasons for your answer.

Exam Questions

Q1 To what extent did the war intensify the problems that faced Tsar Nicholas II? [30 marks]

Q2 Why did the Tsar become increasingly unpopular during the First World War? [30 marks]

Glossary

Zemgor — 'United Committee of the Union of Zemstva and the Union of Towns', a group established to help with the war effort

Haemophilia — an illness where the blood is unable to clot

You can't make everyone happy — but you can make everyone unhappy...

In the exam don't just say that the war was the main cause of the revolution. Consider other factors and say which ones were more important than others. No one answer is right — it's all about arguing your case convincingly. Shhhh... don't tell the mathematicians.

The February Revolution 1917

Public discontent finally reached breaking point during the February Revolution. The armed forces which had supported the Tsar during the 1905 Revolution mutinied and the Tsar was finally overthrown.

There were **Political** and **Social Factors** which helped lead to **Revolution**

Learn these key points:

ECONOMIC & SOCIAL PROBLEMS

- Russian towns were **overcrowded** and had **poor** sanitation and water supplies.
- **Famine** was **common** as food supplies were **unreliable**.
- Living **conditions** for workers were **cramped** and **unhealthy**.
- Men and women worked for **long hours** and for **little pay**.
- **Health** and **education** services were **poor** and created social inequalities.
- In 1914 Russia's **industrial output** was ranked **fifth** out of the five great powers. Smaller countries like Britain and Germany still out-produced Russia.

HOWEVER...

The Russian economy had **grown** massively since the 1890s.

POLITICS

- The Tsar was **reluctant** to give the Duma more **responsibility**.
- Nicholas's **reluctance** to make major reforms **disappointed** many politicians.

HOWEVER...

- By 1914 the **Duma** had become an accepted part of national political life, which shows that the old system of **autocracy** was changing.
- The Duma had a lot of potential to **develop** into a **powerful** force.

TSARIST SYSTEM

Nicholas **wasn't** a very **effective leader**. For example:
- His father, Alexander III, said that his son was **'girlie'**.
- When his father died in 1894 Nicholas admitted that he **didn't feel fit** to **govern**.
- In 1914 Nicholas was strongly **influenced** by his wife Alexandra and Rasputin (see page 19). This had **disastrous** consequences for the Tsar's reputation over the next three years.

HOWEVER...

- In **1913** the Tsar celebrated **300 years** of **Romanov** rule. Nicholas and his family felt confident enough to **parade** through the streets of St. Petersburg **without fear**, which shows that there **wasn't strong opposition** to them.
- This event was **widely** celebrated by the public, which shows that the Tsar's reputation had improved since the 1905 Revolution.

By **January 1917** war had left Russia in a **Critical State**

1) Over a **million** Russian troops were **dead** and **four million** had been **wounded**.
2) Workers in the cities were **suffering** — many were on the verge of **starvation**.
3) The **Okhrana** warned the government about **unrest** and indicated that a **revolution** could happen at any moment.
4) Rodzianko, President of the Duma, **warned** the Tsar that Russia was reaching a **crisis point**. Nicholas **ignored** the warning.

Strikes and **Demonstrations Led** to **Revolution**

1) In **1905** the government had been able to use **force** to disperse rioters and **crush strikes**.
2) In **1917** the situation was different — there was **widespread support** for the strikers **among all classes** in society.
3) Most of the **troops** in Petrograd were **unwilling** to open fire on the protesters.
4) The **wealthier classes** believed that the monarchy couldn't be **saved** (and **wasn't worth** saving anyway).

The February Revolution 1917

Learn the **Key Dates** and **Events** leading up to the **Revolution**

Jan 1917 ⟹ The anniversary of Bloody Sunday was commemorated by very **large demonstrations** in the city.

22nd Feb ⟹ **20 000 workers** from the Putilov engineering works went on **strike** and demonstrated in the city.

23rd Feb ⟹ **International Women's Day** was marked with demonstrations and meetings demanding bread and fuel.

The revolution mostly happened in Petrograd.

25th Feb ⟹ **Petrograd** was **paralysed** by a **general strike** — industry shut down.

27th Feb ⟹ **The strikes and demonstrations turned into a revolution.**
- The Tsar **ordered** the Petrograd troops to **suppress unrest.**
- There was widespread **mutiny** among the troops.
- Nicholas ordered the Duma to **shut down** — they **refused** and set up a **Provisional Committee.**
- The army's High Command **ordered** all troops to **obey** the orders of the **Provisional Committee.**

28th Feb ⟹ A group of left-wing parties set up the **Petrograd Soviet**, which would look after the interests of **workers** and **soldiers.**

A **Chain** of Events Forced Nicholas to Abdicate

28th Feb
1) Nicholas travelled by train towards Petrograd, but his train was **diverted** to Pskov by mutinous troops.
2) Here he met with members of the army's **High Command**, some **ministers**, and representatives of the **Duma.**
3) They told the Tsar that he should **abdicate** in favour of his son **Alexei.**
4) Nicholas feared that his haemophiliac son wouldn't be **strong enough** to rule.

2nd March
1) Nicholas II abdicated and asked his brother **Grand Duke Michael** to become Tsar.
2) Michael **refused** and Romanov rule **ended.**

3rd March
1) The **Provisional Committee** became the **Provisional Government.**
2) It ruled Russia for just **seven** months.

The royal family were placed under **house arrest** and in **summer 1918** the **Bolsheviks murdered** them.

The **February Revolution** took the **Socialist Revolutionaries** by **Surprise**

1) Since the 1880s parties such as the **Socialist Revolutionaries**, the **Bolsheviks** and the **Mensheviks** had **grown** in size and had become more **organised.**
2) But the February Revolution took them by **surprise.** They **failed** to **seize control** of the Revolution.
3) Most of the leading Bolsheviks were **abroad** when it happened. **Stalin** was in exile in Siberia, **Lenin** was in Switzerland and **Trotsky** was in the United States.
4) The only influence the revolutionaries had over the events of February and March was the establishment of the **Petrograd Soviet**, which **shared power** with the **Provisional Government** until October.

Practice Questions

Q1 Draw up a list of the main short-term causes of the 1917 February Revolution.

Exam Question

Q1 Why did the Tsar abdicate in March 1917? [30 marks]

Revolution after revolution after revolution — it's making me feel dizzy...
You may find some different dates for these events. This is because Russia's calendar was 13 days behind the Western calendar until 1918. It won't matter which one you use in the exam though, so just stick to the dates you've been taught.

Introduction to Section 3

I bet you've often wondered, "Where can I find a concise, preferably jazzy, really useful page to help me learn the key dates, key people and historical vocab for the Bolshevik Triumph of 1917?" Well, wonder no more...

Here's a **Quick Summary** of **Section Three**

This section deals with the rule of the Provisional Government between March and October 1917. Here's some useful information:

- The **Provisional Government** wasn't totally in control. It **shared power** with the **Petrograd Soviet**.
- **Lenin's** return to Russia in April **strengthened** the **Bolsheviks** and made them more **popular**.
- Despite the **failure** of the **June Offensive**, the Provisional Government **crushed** the **July Days** rising.
- The **Kornilov affair failed** to topple the government, but in October 1917 the **Bolsheviks** organised a **coup** and **seized power** in Petrograd.

Learn the **Key Dates** of the **Bolshevik Triumph**

The **Provisional Government** ruled Russia between **March** and **October 1917**.

Ahh... those July Days.

March	➡	3rd March — The **First Provisional Government** began.
April	➡	3rd April — **Lenin** returned to Petrograd from exile.
June	➡	The **June Offensive**.
July	➡	The **July Days**. ➡ 8th July — The **Second Provisional Government** began.
August	➡	The **Kornilov affair**.

October ➡

10th October
The **Bolsheviks** decided to **seize power** from the Provisional Government.

➡ **24th October**
The **October Revolution** began.

➡ **26th October**
Lenin announced that the **All-Russian Congress of Soviets** was the new Russian government.

Important people in the Bolshevik Triumph

- **Prince Lvov** — Prime Minister of the First Provisional Government.
- **Alexander Kerensky** — Prime Minister of the Second Provisional Government.
- **Vladimir Lenin** — leader of the Bolshevik Party.
- **Leon Trotsky** — organiser of the October Revolution.
- **General Kornilov** — attempted to overthrow the Provisional Government.

Make sure you know what these **Historical Terms** mean

- **Dual Power** — Shared power between the Petrograd Soviet and the Provisional Government.
- **Constituent Assembly** — A body created to draft a constitution.
- **Soviet** — A council elected by workers.

- **April Theses** — A policy statement of Lenin's calling for revolution.
- **July Days** — A series of demonstrations against the Provisional Government.

Dual Power

This page covers the power-share between the Provisional Government and the Petrograd Soviet after the fall of the Tsar. Things start out promisingly, but it doesn't last long...

The **Provisional Government** and the **Petrograd Soviet Shared Power**

Provisional Government

- The **Provisional Committee** of the Duma took over as the **Provisional Government** led by **Prince Lvov**.
- The government was mainly made up of **Kadets** and other **Liberal** parties.
- The only **socialist** in the government was the Socialist Revolutionary **Alexander Kerensky**.
- The Provisional Government had **no lawful authority**. It hadn't been **appointed** by the Tsar or **elected** by the Russian people.
- It announced that it would govern until a **Constituent Assembly** was elected which would draw up a new **constitution** for the country.
- During its first weeks in power the government had some popular **support** and its authority was **respected** in the larger cities. However, it had **little power** in the provinces.
- Local politicians decided that they would rule **without interference** from the government.

Petrograd Soviet

- The **Petrograd Soviet** was made up of **workers elected** by their **factories**.
- It aimed to look after **workers' interests** and to **protect** their **rights**.
- Workers' and soldiers' soviets were also set up in **other towns**.
- At first the soviets were dominated by **Mensheviks** and **Socialist Revolutionaries**, but the **Bolsheviks** became more **influential**.
- The Petrograd Soviet was worried that the **army** might be used to **crush** the **revolution**, so it passed **Soviet Order Number 1**.

Soviet Order Number 1

- Soldiers could only **obey** military orders if they had been **approved** by the **Petrograd Soviet**.
- This gave the soviet **military** power.

Dual Power Worked Well... for a While

The Provisional Government and the Petrograd Soviet agreed on some early **reforms**:

1) Free **speech** and **freedom of the press**.
2) The **Constituent Assembly** should be **democratically elected**.
3) The **abolition** of the **Okhrana**.
4) All **political prisoners** were **freed**.
5) **Trade unions** were **legally recognised**.
6) The **abolition** of the **death penalty** (although it was brought back for the **armed forces** later in the year).

Although these reforms were **impressive**, they didn't tackle the **huge problems** the country still faced. Both sides wanted the **war** to go on. The Provisional Government wanted to leave the problem of **land reform** to the **Constituent Assembly**.

Practice Question

Q1   List three early reforms agreed upon by the Provisional Government and the Petrograd Soviet.

Glossary

The Constituent Assembly — a group of elected representatives who would agree on the rules by which a new government would be elected.

The Provisional Government was in trouble from the start...

The main problem with the Provisional Government was that it was formed of middle-class politicians, who had no idea what working-class people wanted. For instance, they decided to carry on in World War I, even though everyone else had had enough.

Opposition to the Provisional Government

You need to know the importance of Lenin, and about the impact he had on the Bolsheviks and their struggle for power. Lenin was a strong leader, who had a way of appealing to ordinary Russians, which made him very popular.

There were **Conflicting Attitudes** towards the **War**

Socialist Parties
- Wanted a **defensive** war.
- Thought the army shouldn't **advance** against the enemy but should **prevent** the Germans from advancing into **Russia**.

Kadets and Liberals
- Wanted to **continue** fighting.
- Believed that Russia had an **obligation** towards its **allies**.
- Peace with Germany would mean **loss** of **land** and national **humiliation**.

Bolsheviks
- Wanted a **defensive** war until Lenin came back.
- **Lenin** demanded an immediate **end** to the war.
- This policy became very **popular** between **April** and **October 1917**.

The Provisional Government was dominated by the **Kadets** and **Liberals**, so it decided to **continue** the war. Ministers also knew that the Russian **economy** depended on **allied loans**, so they'd **lose money** if they pulled out of the war.

Lenin was the **Leader** of the **Bolsheviks**

- Lenin was born in **1870** into a **middle-class** family.
- A key moment in his early life was when his **brother** Alexander was **executed** for taking part in an 1887 plot to **assassinate** Tsar Alexander III.
- He became a **political revolutionary** and took on **Marxist** ideas at **university**.
- Lenin spent most of his adult life in **exile**.

© Mary Evans Picture Library

Vladimir Lenin (1870-1924)

Lenin Wanted the Soviets to Seize Power

1) The **February Revolution** took Lenin by **surprise** — he was in **Switzerland** at the time.
2) The German government helped him to get back to Russia because they hoped that the Bolsheviks would work to **undermine** Russia's war efforts.
3) Since the Tsar had abdicated, the **Bolsheviks** had been working with other socialist parties and had **supported** the Provisional Government. Lenin changed all that.
4) He arrived in Petrograd on **3rd April** and declared his **complete opposition** to the **government** — calling for an **immediate socialist revolution**. He set out his programme for the Bolsheviks in his **April Theses**.

> The **April Theses** called for:
> 1) A **revolution** to **seize power** from the **Provisional Government** and transfer it to the **Soviets**.
> 2) An immediate **end** to the **war**.
> 3) The transfer of all **land** to the **peasants**.
>
> Lenin summed up his aims with two **slogans**: **All Power to the Soviets** **Peace, Bread, Land**

Lenin Strengthened Support for the Bolsheviks

1) Before Lenin came back the Bolsheviks **competed** with other left-wing parties for public support.
2) Lenin's **radical demands** meant that the Bolsheviks appeared **distinct** and **different**.
3) They **attracted support** from people who were against the **war** and who felt **let down** by the Provisional Government.
4) The **peasants** were attracted to Lenin's policy of **land reforms**, and they **switched** from the **SRs** to the **Bolsheviks**.

Opposition to the Provisional Government

Although the war had been one of the factors which had led to the fall of Tsarism, there were still disagreements about how Russia should deal with it. The bit about the June Offensive is pretty important, so read on...

The **Milyukov Crisis Changed** the **Government**

1) In April **1917** the Foreign Minister **Milyukov** secretly informed the Allies that Russia would **stay in the war**. He expected Russia to gain **territory** from Turkey if there was an Allied **victory**.
2) In **April** news of Milyukov's proposals were **leaked** — there were **violent demonstrations** in Petrograd.
3) In **May** Milyukov **resigned** and Prince Lvov made **major changes** to the government.
4) The **Mensheviks** and **SRs** joined the government, and **Kerensky** was appointed **Minister of War**.

The **June Offensive** was a **Disaster** for the **Provisional Government**

Kerensky believed that an **offensive** campaign against the Germans would **unite** the country behind the war and **increase support** for the Provisional Government.

- The **June Offensive** of 1917 was an attack led by **Brusilov** against Austro-Hungarian and German forces.
- It was Russia's last great effort in the war and was a complete **disaster**.
- Official figures suggested that **400 000** soldiers **died** and **170 000 deserted** — the real figures are probably much **higher**.
- The **army** was beginning to **disintegrate**. Troops **mutinied** and **desertions** were **widespread**.
- Many soldiers were influenced by **Bolshevik agitators** and had **lost** the **will** to fight.

The **July Days Strengthened** the **Provisional Government**

1) The **failure** of the June Offensive triggered the **July Days** — a period of **rioting** and **violence** in Petrograd.
2) It's unclear whether **Lenin** ordered the rioting in Petrograd. However, many Bolshevik leaders felt it was the **beginning** of a full-blown **revolution** and they wanted to take advantage of it.
3) The uprising was **badly led** and **disorganised**.
4) After just three days the Provisional Government used loyal troops to **restore order**.
5) The Provisional Government's ability to **crush** the uprising **reinforced** its **authority** and restored some of its **control** over Russia.

Practice Questions

Q1 Discuss how the main parties' attitudes to Russia's participation in World War I differed.

Q2 Explain why many ordinary Russians supported Lenin and the Bolsheviks.

Q3 Why would the phrases 'All power to the Soviets' and 'Peace, Bread, Land' appeal to the Russian people?

Q4 Summarise why the June Offensive was so disastrous to the Provisional Government.

Q5 What was more damaging to the Provisional Government — the July Days or the June Offensive?

Learn plenty of facts and figures to include in your essays...

There's nothing too tricky to remember here — just make sure you're clear on what the Socialists, Provisional Government and Bolsheviks aimed to do, how the people of Russia felt about it, and how Lenin managed to win support from the working classes.

The Provisional Government in Crisis

Successfully crushing the July Days may have made it seem that the Provisional Government was getting control of the situation. But another crisis was just around the corner.

The July Days **Weakened** the **Bolsheviks...** but not **Fatally**

1) After the July Days, the government **moved against** the Bolsheviks and **claimed** that Lenin was a **traitor**.

2) Leading Bolsheviks were **arrested** — Lenin **fled to Finland**.

3) Some Bolsheviks thought that the events of July were a **massive defeat** and the party wouldn't be able to **recover**.

1) **Bolshevik support** was **increasing** — especially among the **army** and the **peasants**.

2) Although the government **weakened** the Bolsheviks in the short term, they **didn't** attempt to **destroy** the **Bolsheviks** altogether.

The **Second Provisional Government** was led by **Alexander Kerensky**

1) In July Prince Lvov **resigned** as leader of the Provisional Government and a **second** government was formed.

2) **Alexander Kerensky** became Prime Minister, heading a government of SRs, Kadets, Progressives and Mensheviks.

3) He got rid of **Brusilov** and appointed **General Kornilov** as Commander-in-Chief.

4) Kornilov reintroduced the death penalty for **deserters** and **mutineers**, to **restore discipline** in the army.

5) Kerensky's government faced some serious **economic** and **agricultural problems**:

Economic Problems

1) **Inflation** got **worse**. Rises in **workers' wages didn't** match the **rise** in **prices**. Workers started to **strike**.

2) The government couldn't **provide** enough **food** and **fuel** to the towns and cities.

3) The peasants **refused** to sell their **grain** because money was essentially **worthless**. As a result, the daily allowance of **bread** in Petrograd **fell** between July and November 1917.

4) **Fuel shortages** forced factories, including **munitions** works, to **close**. The army then had to deal with **inadequate supplies** as well as **desertions**.

Agricultural Problems

1) The **peasants** believed that the **Tsar's land** would be given to them. They were **angered** by the Provisional Government's decision to **ignore** the issue until the Constituent Assembly was **elected**.

2) Peasant **militancy** was **strengthened** by deserting **soldiers** returning to their villages, and by others on leave.

3) **Violence** towards **landowners** became widespread — many were **killed** and their land was **seized**.

The **Kornilov Affair Weakened** the **Provisional Government**...

1) In August General Kornilov ordered troops to march on the **capital**, where it was believed he wanted to **overthrow** the government and rule as a **military dictator**.

2) Kerensky **panicked** and joined forces with the **Petrograd Soviet** in an attempt to **resist** Kornilov and **defend** the revolution.

3) **Arms** and **ammunition** were issued to **workers** and the capital prepared for Kornilov's attack.

4) The rebellion **collapsed**, and Kornilov was **dismissed** and **arrested**.

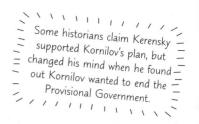

Some historians claim Kerensky supported Kornilov's plan, but changed his mind when he found out Kornilov wanted to end the Provisional Government.

The Provisional Government in Crisis

... but Strengthened the Bolsheviks

1) Leading Bolsheviks were **released** from prison and given **weapons** to defend the city from Kornilov.
2) In September they gained **control** of the Petrograd Soviet, which strengthened their position.
3) Army officers believed that Kerensky was a **weak leader** who had given in to revolutionary groups. As a result they **refused** to **support** the government during the **October Revolution**.
4) The Kornilov Affair showed the Bolsheviks that the government now had **little support** and could be **easily overthrown**. Support for the Bolsheviks grew — they gained **majorities** in the **Petrograd** and **Moscow Soviets**.
5) The Bolshevik's slogan '**Peace, Bread, Land**' increased their popularity with **peasants** and **soldiers**.
6) Kerensky felt **threatened** — he **shut down** the party's **printing presses** and **arrested** leading party members.

The Timing of the 1917 October Revolution was Crucial

Lenin learnt from the **July Days** that a **premature** and **unplanned** attempt to overthrow the Provisional Government would only end in failure. But by October he was convinced that a second, **well-planned** rising would **succeed**.

1) Lenin returned in **October** and convinced the Bolshevik Central Committee to begin an **immediate armed uprising**.
2) He wanted to seize power in the name of the **Soviets** when the **All-Russian Congress of Soviets** met in **October**.
3) The Provisional Government announced that **elections** for the **Constituent Assembly** would be held in **November**.
4) Lenin feared the **SRs** would gain the most seats, and he didn't want to **share** power with any other political party.
5) **Leon Trotsky** led the Soviet's **Military Revolutionary Committee** which carried out the rising.

24th Oct	• **Trotsky** ordered the Bolshevik Red Guards to **seize** key positions within **Petrograd**. • They took over the **railway** stations, and the **post** and **telegraph** offices.
25th Oct	• Kerensky fled to try and organise a **counter-attack** using **loyal troops**. • His attempt at resistance **failed**, and he **left** the country. • The Bolsheviks **stormed** the Winter Palace where the government was meeting and **arrested** the **ministers** without a fight.
26th Oct	• Lenin announced to the **All-Russian Congress of Soviets** that the Provisional Government had been **overthrown** and that **power** was transferred to the **Congress**. • The Congress handed power over to a **Council of People's Commissars**, chaired by **Lenin**.

Within a few weeks the Bolsheviks had gained **control** over important cities and begun **communist rule**.

Practice Questions

Q1 Briefly summarise the importance of the July Days.

Q2 'The Kornilov Affair helped the Bolsheviks seize power in 1917.' Do you agree with this statement?

Exam Question

Q1 Why did the 1917 October Revolution succeed? [30 marks]

Kerensky was pretty much doomed from the start...

Poor old Kerensky — he's finally got his dream job and it's turning into a nightmare. Not only has he acquired the leadership of a country where people are starving and striking, but the man he trusted to sort out the army turns out to be plotting against him too.

Introduction to Section 4

Yes, you've guessed it — it's that part of the book again where you get a page dedicated to making your life better.
Get learning those key dates, key people and historical vocab. But have a cup of tea first.

Here's a **Quick Summary** of **Section Four**

This section deals with the years **1917-24**, when the Bolsheviks defeated
all their **domestic** and **foreign enemies** and **established** their **power** in Russia.

Here's some information to get you started:

- The new **Bolshevik** government made **peace** with **Germany** at **Brest-Litovsk** in **March 1918**.
- The **Red Army crushed** the Whites during the **Civil War**.
- **Lenin** introduced a series of **economic reforms** to fix Russia's **struggling** economy.
- By the time of **Lenin's death** in **1924**, Bolshevik **control** over Russia was **complete**.

Learn the **Key Dates** of the **Bolshevik's Campaign**

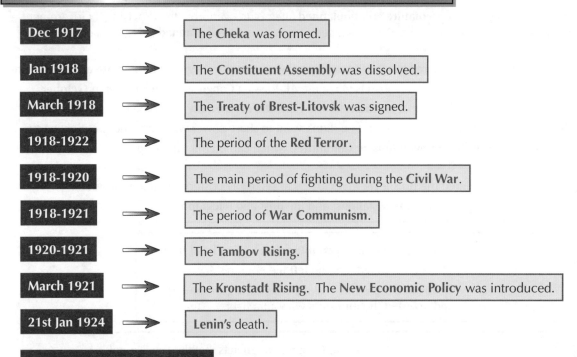

Dec 1917 ⟹	The **Cheka** was formed.
Jan 1918 ⟹	The **Constituent Assembly** was dissolved.
March 1918 ⟹	The **Treaty of Brest-Litovsk** was signed.
1918-1922 ⟹	The period of the **Red Terror**.
1918-1920 ⟹	The main period of fighting during the **Civil War**.
1918-1921 ⟹	The period of **War Communism**.
1920-1921 ⟹	The **Tambov Rising**.
March 1921 ⟹	The **Kronstadt Rising**. The **New Economic Policy** was introduced.
21st Jan 1924 ⟹	**Lenin's** death.

Important People in this Period:

- **Felix Dzerzhinsky** — leader of the Cheka.
- **General Denikin** — leader of the Whites in southern Russia.
- **Admiral Kolchak** — leader of the Whites in Siberia.
- **General Yudenich** — leader of the Whites in the Baltic States.

Make sure you know what these **Historical Terms** mean

- **Cheka** — The Bolsheviks' secret police force.
- **Reds** — The name of the Bolsheviks' military force.
- **Whites** — The name given to the anti-Bolshevik forces.
- **State Capitalism** — The first Bolshevik economic policy, which avoided making big changes.

- **War Communism** — The Bolsheviks' economic policy during the Civil War — party control of industry, grain requisitioning, and a ban on private enterprise.
- **New Economic Policy** — The policy introduced after War Communism to prevent economic collapse — reintroduced some private enterprise.

The Bolsheviks Take Control (1917-1918)

The Bolsheviks' rise to power was relatively easy, but they were now faced with some serious challenges. Lenin found out that with great power comes great responsibility. And he didn't have any 'Spidey senses' to help him out...

The **Bolsheviks'** position was **Weak**

Although the Bolsheviks successfully **overthrew** the **government**, they had to **strengthen** their **hold** on Russia:

1) Russia was **still at war** with Germany and Austria-Hungary. The Bolsheviks had to **end** this conflict **before** it **destroyed** Russia and the new government.

2) The **Socialist Revolutionaries** (SRs) were **far more popular** than the Bolsheviks.

3) Although Moscow and other cities in Russia fell into Bolshevik hands, Lenin had **little political control** over the rest of Russia.

4) The Bolsheviks also needed to bring **economic stability** to Russia.

The Bolsheviks came **Second** in the 1917 **Election**

The October Revolution came **too late** to **stop elections** which were scheduled for **November 12th 1917**:

1) Lenin felt he **couldn't** afford to **risk unpopularity** so soon after seizing power, so he **allowed** the **12th November election** to go ahead.

2) The elections were the **freest** and most **democratic** that had ever been held in Russia.

3) **Men** and **women** aged **21** or over were entitled to **vote**.

4) The Bolsheviks were **heavily beaten** in the election by the SRs.

> **Election Results:**
>
> The SRs won 370 seats.
> The Bolsheviks won 175.
>
> The SRs won 21 million votes.
> The Bolsheviks won 9 million.

Lenin **Shut Down** the Constituent Assembly

Lenin had **no faith** in **democracy** and a non-Bolshevik controlled Constituent Assembly could pose major problems.

The End of the Constituent Assembly

1) During the election campaign Lenin **spoke against** the Constituent Assembly. He argued that the **existence** of the **All-Russian Congress of Soviets** meant that the **Assembly** was **unnecessary**. Lenin also **claimed** there was **widespread corruption** during the election, but he had **no proof**.

2) The Constituent Assembly met in Petrograd on **5th January 1918** and the delegates held a **long** and **heated debate**. At **4am** on **6th January** the tired guards **asked** the delegates **to leave**.

3) When the delegates **returned**, later that morning, the **Assembly** had been **dissolved** on the orders of the government and the delegates were **dispersed** at **gunpoint**.

4) The dissolving of the Constituent Assembly was an **early sign** that the Bolsheviks **weren't prepared** to **share power** with any of the political parties.

Practice Questions

Q1   Summarise why the Bolsheviks' control was so weak in 1917.

Q2   Briefly explain why the 1917 election was problematic for the Bolsheviks.

In the exam please don't make any spleling mistakes...

Write down all the names of the important people in this period, cover them up and then try to spell them. Make sure you remember what they did as well. This is the last section, so you might as well do one long test with all of the names... Fun, fun, fun.

The Bolsheviks Take Control (1917-1918)

Lenin had to escape the war or risk losing everything he had fought so hard to get — even if this would cost Russia dearly. He didn't want to make the same mistakes as his predecessors in power.

Lenin **Had** to get Russia **Out** of the **War**

1) Russia's involvement in the First World War had been a **major factor** in both the **fall** of **Tsarism** and in the **overthrow** of the **Provisional Government**.

2) Lenin knew that the **Bolshevik government** had to pull out of the war to avoid the same thing happening to them.

3) The **first act** of the Bolshevik government was to issue the **Decree on Peace**, which called for an **immediate end** to the **war**.

4) The Russian army **couldn't continue** to fight — Lenin ordered a **ceasefire**.

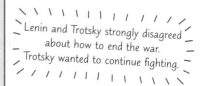

Lenin and Trotsky strongly disagreed about how to end the war. Trotsky wanted to continue fighting.

The **Treaty** of **Brest-Litovsk** was **Humiliating** for Russia

Lenin wanted a **peace agreement** with Germany and Austria-Hungary, at any **cost**.

1) **Trotsky**, who was Commissar for Foreign Affairs, went to **Brest-Litovsk** to **negotiate** a **peace treaty** with Germany and Austria-Hungary.

2) The Central Powers **weren't prepared** to **negotiate** with Trotsky. Instead they demanded to **impose** their **own terms**.

Trotsky at Brest-Litovsk

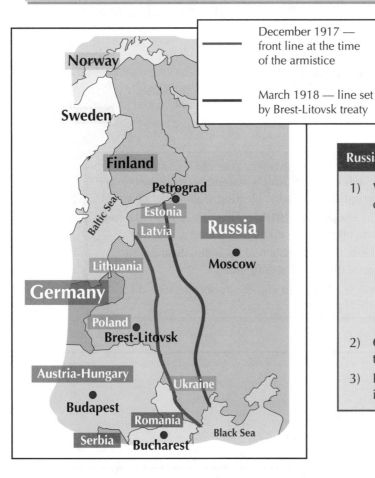

December 1917 — front line at the time of the armistice

March 1918 — line set by Brest-Litovsk treaty

Russia Lost...

1) **Vast areas** of land in the western part of the country, including:
   - Finland
   - Latvia
   - Estonia
   - Lithuania
   - Poland
   - Ukraine

2) **One third** of its agricultural land, including the **fertile** grain-producing areas in **Ukraine**.

3) **Half** of its heavy industry and nearly **90%** of its **coal mines**, mostly in the **Donbass region**.

Lenin was prepared to **accept** such a **harsh treaty**, because Russia couldn't continue to fight in the war. He also knew that Russia might be able to **claim back** some of the land if Germany **lost** the war.

The Bolsheviks Take Control (1917-1918)

Lenin had seen how easy it was to seize power in Russia, so he had to make sure that the Bolsheviks weren't overthrown themselves. He created a new secret police force to suppress anyone who didn't agree with him.

Lenin created the **Cheka** to keep **Order** in Russia

1) In **December 1917** the **Okhrana** was **replaced** by the **Extraordinary Commission for Combating Counter-Revolution and Sabotage** — better known as the **Cheka**.

2) The Cheka was far **more efficient** than the Okhrana. Its main **aims** were to **maintain state security** and **ensure** the **continuation** of **Bolshevik rule**.

3) The Cheka soon established itself **outside** of the **law**. It had the **power** to arrest, prosecute, imprison and execute **any** real or suspected **enemies** of the government.

Russian people hated the Cheka for **two** main **reasons**:

1) They set up **concentration camps** where people were forced to **work** as **slave labour**.

2) They formed **grain requisition squads** to seize **grain** from the **peasants**.

Many of Lenin's **Opponents** were **Persecuted** in the **Red Terror**

1) In the summer of **1918**, **two assassination** attempts on **Lenin** gave **Felix Dzerzhinsky** (the head of Cheka) the excuse to unleash the **Red Terror**.

2) Thousands of Russians were rounded up and **executed** for **anti-Bolshevik activity**, including many members of **opposition parties**.

3) **Priests** were targeted as 'enemies of the people' in a sustained attack on the **Orthodox Church**. Churches were **looted** and **destroyed**.

4) Many people were **executed** for being **aristocrats** or members of the **middle class**.

5) In **July 1918** the former **Tsar Nicholas** and his **entire family** were **murdered** on Lenin's **orders**. Lenin feared that the Tsar could become a **figurehead** for the **opposition** to **rally** around.

6) The **Red Terror** came to an **end** in **1922**. It's estimated that up to **500 000** Russians died.

By the **summer** of **1918** the Bolsheviks' **hold** on government was **strengthening**, but they still **weren't** in **complete control** of Russia. **Opposition** forces began to **raise armies** of their own and Russia was **plunged** into a **Civil War**.

Practice Questions

Q1 How important for the Bolshevik government was the making of peace with Germany?

Q2 Evaluate whether the Treaty of Brest-Litovsk was beneficial to Russia.

Q3 Describe the Bolsheviks' approach to dealing with political opposition in the years after the October Revolution.

Exam Question

Q1 How successful were the Bolsheviks in dealing with opposition from November 1917 to June 1918? [30 Marks]

In the chess game that was Russia — the secret police were Cheka-Mate...

Lenin's use of force was pretty terrifying, but it was ultimately effective. He needed to secure his position quickly, as a civil war seemed to be on its way. By persecuting and executing opponents, he was able to put himself firmly in control. Once the Bolshevik regime was secure, they were able to organise and launch a powerful military campaign when the war came.

Civil War and Foreign Intervention (1918-1921)

The Bolsheviks' attempts to establish power after the October Revolution were met with strong opposition. The Reds and the Whites fought each other in a vicious and bloody Civil War. Sounds a bit like the North London Derby...

Resistance to the Bolsheviks was both *Domestic* and *Foreign*

Opposition to the Bolsheviks came from **several sources**, which **together** became known as the **White Armies**.

1) The **SRs** and the **Mensheviks** were angry at not being **included** in the government and **opposed a one-party state**. The **1917 election** proved that the SRs were by far the **largest** party in Russia and they were determined to gain political power.

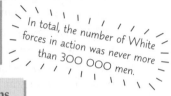

In total, the number of White forces in action was never more than 300 000 men.

2) Some national **minorities**, especially the **Finns, Poles and Ukrainians**, wanted **self-government**. They became known as the **Greens**.

3) Several **counter-revolutionary groups** wanted to **restore** the **Provisional Government**. Other counter-revolutionaries wanted to bring back **Tsarist** rule.

4) Russia's apparent **betrayal** of their **western allies** through the **Treaty of Brest-Litovsk** led Britain, France, Japan and the US to **invade** and **occupy** parts of the country.

5) The **Czech Legion** was a force of over **60 000** men. They were created by the **Tsar** to fight the Central Powers and their aim was to form an **independent state**. After the war, they were allowed to return home, via **Vladivostok**, on the **Trans-Siberian Railway**. However, they were encouraged by **Britain** and the **US** to **fight** the **Bolsheviks**. It was this that triggered off the main fighting of the **Civil War** in **June/July 1918**.

6) In Ukraine, **Nestor Makhno** led an **anti-Bolshevik army** called the **Black Army**.

The *Whites* were *Scattered* across Russia

1) **Supporters** of the former **Tsar** and the **Provisional Government** were grouped in southern Russia. They were commanded by **General Denikin**.
2) **Various groups** in **Siberia** came together under **Admiral Kolchak**.
3) **Opposition forces** in the **Baltic States** were led by **General Yudenich**.
4) The **Czech Legion** controlled the **Trans-Siberian Railway**.

Look at them scattering! There are so many... we're all going to die! We're - oh wait, I just spilt my mints.

Bolshevik forces were known as the *Red Army*

- The **Russian army**, which had been at war with Germany and Austria-Hungary, had **fallen apart**. Trotsky had to **rebuild** it to **defend** the **Revolution**.
- The army **grew** from a few hundred thousand men in early 1918 to **5 million** in **1920**.

Civil War and Foreign Intervention (1918-1921)

At first the Bolsheviks looked like they were in trouble — just look at the pretty map below... It didn't look too good for Lenin and the gang, but with a little bit of Trotsky's genius they powered on through to victory. Onward comrades...

The **Red Army** won the Civil War **Quickly**

1919 was the crucial year of the Civil War. The Red Army began the year being **pushed back**. However, Trotsky focused on picking off each opposing army **one by one**. By the **end** of **1919** the Civil War was effectively **won**.

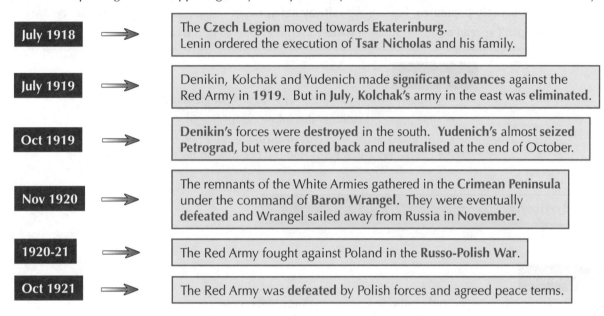

July 1918 ⟹	The **Czech Legion** moved towards **Ekaterinburg**. Lenin ordered the execution of **Tsar Nicholas** and his family.
July 1919 ⟹	Denikin, Kolchak and Yudenich made **significant advances** against the Red Army in **1919**. But in **July**, **Kolchak's** army in the east was **eliminated**.
Oct 1919 ⟹	**Denikin's** forces were **destroyed** in the south. **Yudenich's** almost **seized Petrograd**, but were **forced back** and **neutralised** at the end of October.
Nov 1920 ⟹	The remnants of the White Armies gathered in the **Crimean Peninsula** under the command of **Baron Wrangel**. They were eventually **defeated** and Wrangel sailed away from Russia in **November**.
1920-21 ⟹	The Red Army fought against Poland in the **Russo-Polish War**.
Oct 1921 ⟹	The Red Army was **defeated** by Polish forces and agreed peace terms.

The Whites **Surrounded** the Reds

Despite being **surrounded**, the Reds were in a much **stronger position** than the Whites.

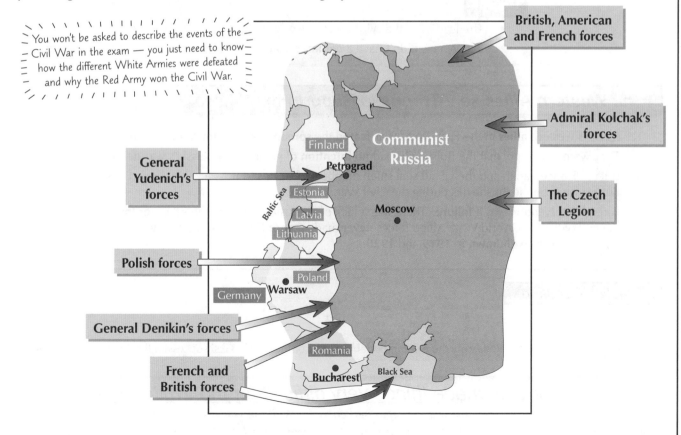

You won't be asked to describe the events of the Civil War in the exam — you just need to know how the different White Armies were defeated and why the Red Army won the Civil War.

British, American and French forces

Admiral Kolchak's forces

The Czech Legion

General Yudenich's forces

Polish forces

General Denikin's forces

French and British forces

Finland · Petrograd · Baltic Sea · Estonia · Latvia · Lithuania · Moscow · Poland · Warsaw · Germany · Romania · Bucharest · Black Sea · **Communist Russia**

Civil War and Foreign Intervention (1918-1921)

The Red Army had **Two** main **Advantages**

They were:

Geographical Position

- The Bolsheviks only controlled about **15%** of the territory of the **old Russian Empire**.
- But this area was **densely populated**, had a good **railway network** and it included major **industrial centres**.
- The Red Army **wasn't spread out**. This made it **harder** for the Whites to find **weaknesses**.

Lenin's policy of War Communism made sure that the army was well fed and supplied with arms.

Leon Trotsky

- Trotsky created the Red Army almost **single-handedly**.
- He imposed **ruthless discipline** on his troops.
- Trotsky's leadership was **inspiring** and he raised the morale of soldiers when he visited the frontline in his armoured train.

The White Army had **Two** main **Disadvantages**

They were:

Geographical Position

- The White armies were **separated** from one another by **huge distances**. They often were **unable** to **coordinate** attacks against the Bolsheviks.
- They **controlled** large **rural areas**, but were **unable** to gain the support of the **peasants**, who **feared** the Whites would **bring back** their former **landlords**.

Disunity

- The leaders of the Whites **never worked together** to develop a strategy.
- The Whites **didn't** have a **common cause** — they only shared a hatred for the Bolsheviks.

The **Western Allies** sent **Troops** to **Support** the Whites

1) Russia's **western allies** in the First World War **feared** the **spread** of **communism** in Europe after the war.
2) They were also angry that the Bolsheviks had **no intention** of **paying back** Russia's **war debts**.
3) Britain, France, Japan and the US all sent small numbers of **troops** to Russia. They hoped this would **put pressure** on the Bolsheviks during the Civil War.
4) Foreign intervention was a **failure**. There was a lack of enthusiasm among the Allies for the conflict after the end of the First World War. Allied forces **never** made a **coordinated attempt** to **defeat** the Red Army. The troops were **withdrawn** in **1919** and **1920**.

Practice Question

Exam Question

Q1 To what extent was the Red Army the most important reason for the Bolsheviks' success in the Civil War? [30 Marks]

Trotsky's leadership made things very difficult for the White forces...

The Whites had no chance — they just weren't organised enough. With the war over and done with, Lenin could now turn to dealing with Russia's pressing economic problems. It wasn't an easy ride for the Bolsheviks... not by a long shot.

Bolshevik Economic Policies (1917-1924)

In the middle of fighting a civil war and purging about 500 000 people, the Bolsheviks found time to put together some economic policies. Lenin had promised bread and land, so now he had to try to deliver them.

State Capitalism — more of the Same... but with Some Changes

1) In **October 1917**, the Russian economy was in **poor condition**. Food supplies **weren't** reaching the towns in **sufficient quantities**, the transport system **didn't work** and inflation was **destroying** the **value** of **money**.

2) Lenin's priority was to save Russia's failing economy. He **couldn't** make revolutionary changes to the economy **until** Russia had **pulled out** of the **war** and the **Bolsheviks** had greater **control** over Russia.

3) However, Lenin did make some changes:

   - The **Decree on Land confiscated** all land from existing owners and **distributed** it among the **peasants**.
   - The land decree **didn't** ease food shortages. In fact it made the situation **worse** because the peasants were **too poor** to afford modern machinery and fertilisers to farm the land **efficiently**.
   - The **Decree on Workers' Control** allowed workers to control and run the factories **without supervision**.
   - However, the workers were **unable** to run the factories **efficiently**. Production **fell** even **more**.

4) In **December 1917** the government established the **Supreme Council of the National Economy** (VSNKh). It was charged with **modernising** the country. It **achieved little** until the end of the Civil War in 1921.

War Communism Replaced the existing system

1) When the Civil War broke out in the summer of 1918, Lenin **abandoned** the policy of **State Capitalism**.

2) In its place he established **War Communism**, which was a policy of manipulating the economy in the interests of the army. It had a **major effect** on Russia's **industry** and **agriculture**:

Industry

1) **Industry** came under increased **government control**. The **Decree on Nationalisation** of **June 1918** led to **all** industry being **nationalised** (owned by the state) within **two years**.

2) **Private enterprise** was made **illegal**.

3) **Worker-controlled** factories were **abolished**, and many factories were put under their old management.

4) **Strikes** were made **illegal** and worker **discipline** was **tightened**.

5) During the Civil War, the whole **economy** was **geared** to the **needs** of the **Red Army**. **Non-essential** industries were **unable** to **function** efficiently and **output declined**.

6) The situation was made **worse** by a serious **shortage** of **manpower** due to the Civil War.

In 1918-20, Moscow's population halved and Petrograd's fell by 75%.

Agriculture

1) The government believed that **peasants**, especially the **kulaks**, were **hoarding grain** in order to **force prices** to **rise**. Lenin permitted the use of **force** to **requisition grain**.

2) Grain **requisition squads** went to villages to **seize** any grain they could find. Any **resistance** was put down **brutally** and many peasants were **shot**.

3) The forced requisitioning of grain was **unsuccessful**. Peasants saw **no point** in growing more food than their family needed. As a result agricultural production **fell steeply**.

Bolshevik Economic Policies (1917-1924)

War Communism was incredibly harsh on ordinary Russians. But Lenin needed to do something — he had to keep his troops well supplied. For most people though, it was too much, too fast — it wasn't long before unrest broke out again...

War Communism *Achieved* its *Main Aim* — but at *Great Cost*

War Communism provided sufficient **food** and **supplies** for the **Red Army**.
This contributed to the Bolshevik **success** in the Civil War. But...

1) By **1920**, **inflation** had made money **worthless**.
2) Most **wages** for factory workers were paid in **goods** rather than money.
3) A **black market** in food and goods flourished in most towns and cities.
4) The transport system **collapsed**. Hardly any trains were working, which made it harder to supply towns and cities with food.
5) In **1921**, **famine** gripped large areas of Russia. Between **five** and **ten million** Russians died, and the government was forced to ask for **aid** from **America**.

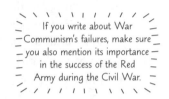

If you write about War Communism's failures, make sure you also mention its importance in the success of the Red Army during the Civil War.

War Communism caused *Disagreements* among the Bolsheviks

1) **Despite** the **hardships** that War Communism inflicted on Russia, many Bolsheviks wanted to **continue** the policy after the Civil War ended.
2) Lenin **agreed** with **radical** Bolsheviks who saw the policy as part of a strategy to establish a **Communist Russia**.
3) Other Bolsheviks **opposed** it. A **Workers' Opposition** was formed, which **campaigned** for an **end** to the policy.

Lenin *Changed* his *Mind* after two *Major Rebellions*

War Communism's unpopularity posed a **threat** to **Lenin** and the **Bolsheviks**.

Tambov Rising

- In **1920-21**, **thousands** of peasants in **Tambov Province** rebelled in **resistance** to **grain requisitioning**.
- The rising was **well organised** and **effectively led**.
- It took **100 000** soldiers, led by **Tukhachevsky**, **several months** to **suppress** the uprising.

Kronstadt Rising

- In **1921**, **thousands** of **workers** and **sailors** gathered at the **Kronstadt** naval base near **Petrograd**.
- They demanded an **immediate** end to War Communism and **greater political freedoms**.
- Trotsky ordered **thousands** of **troops** to attack the base and the rising was **put down** after **savage** fighting.
- The **rebellion** at **Kronstadt** was a **symbolic blow** for the **Bolsheviks** because the **sailors** of **Kronstadt** had **famously helped** the **Bolsheviks' revolution** in **1917**.

Lenin said that the Kronstadt Rising was "the flash that lit up reality". He realised that War Communism **couldn't continue** in its existing form, so he **replaced** it with the **New Economic Policy** (see page 37).

Bolshevik Economic Policies (1917-1924)

The unpopularity of War Communism was a blow for Lenin, but he couldn't risk ignoring public opinion if the Bolsheviks were to stay in power. A Russian economy based only on communist principles would have to wait, for now...

The New Economic Policy — Communism with a Touch of Capitalism

In **March 1921**, Lenin announced to the **10th Party Congress** that War Communism would **end** and Russia would **return** to **some** capitalist methods in agriculture and industry. The main features of the **New Economic Policy** (NEP) were:

1) Many **small-scale** industries were **returned** to their **former owners**.
2) Heavy industry, transport and banks **remained** under **strict state control**.
3) Grain requisitioning **ended** and was **replaced** by a **small tax**, paid in grain.
4) Peasants were allowed to **sell surplus** food at newly established markets.
5) The rouble was **revalued**, bringing back some economic **stability**.
6) **Private trading** was **permitted**.

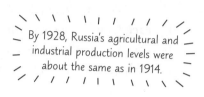
By 1928, Russia's agricultural and industrial production levels were about the same as in 1914.

The NEP was Good for Russia...

1) **Without** grain requisitioning, agricultural **output soared**.
2) The **grain** harvest almost **doubled** between **1921** and **1925**.
3) Industrial output **recovered rapidly**, especially in **raw materials** and **heavy industry**.

The NEP was a **great success**. The Russian economy **recovered** after years of war, revolution and civil war.

... but it led to Divisions amongst the Bolsheviks

The NEP **split** the Bolsheviks into two camps:

Supporters of the NEP

Nikolai Bukharin and other Bolsheviks felt the NEP should last for **many years**. They felt Russia's economy needed to **grow** more **rapidly**.

Opponents of the NEP

Trotsky led **resistance** to the NEP. He feared it was a **return** to **capitalism**. The rise of **Nepmen** (traders who made large profits) and **kulaks** made him **uneasy**.

In **January 1924** Lenin suffered a **stroke** and died. His body was **embalmed** and **displayed** in a **mausoleum** in **Moscow's Red Square**.

Practice Questions

Q1 Explain in what way each economic policy was suited to the conditions in which it was introduced.

Exam Question

Q1 To what extent was War Communism successful in achieving its aims? [30 marks]

Glossary

War Communism — a series of harsh economic measures, brought in to help the war effort. The most important aspect was the requisition of grain.

Here endeth the Lenin...

Yes that's the end of the learnin', now you got to do the churnin'. Obviously, I mean the churnin' out of answers. The next two sections are all about exam technique, types of questions and how to answer them. I hope you enjoy them as much as I do — Yippee...

The Exam

Your exam is Unit 1 — Historical Themes in Breadth — Option D — A World Divided: Communism and Democracy in the 20th Century. A bit of a mouthful. Polar bears don't do exams, but if they did, they'd be brrrrilliant...

You have to answer *Two Questions* in *1 Hour 20 Minutes*

1) The exam paper has questions on **seven topics**. You will have **studied two** of them, so you can **ignore** the rest.

2) You need to know the **name** and **number** of the **topics** you have studied, e.g. D3 — Russia in Revolution, 1881-1924: From Autocracy to Dictatorship.

3) **Each** topic has a choice of **two questions** — you only need to answer **one** of them.

4) The exam is **1 hour 20 minutes**, which gives you **40 minutes per question**.

5) **Each question** is worth **30 marks** — so they're **equally important**.

Great hair gave Tim the confidence to ace his exam.

Don't Rush — *Read* the question and *Plan* your answer

At the start of the Exam

• Look at **both** questions **carefully** and decide which you will find **easier** to answer. Read the **whole question** and not just the key words — the question might be different to what you were expecting.

• Spend about **5 minutes thinking** about what the question is asking you for. Jot down **important points**.

During the Exam

• **Answer the question**. Don't write an answer to a question you've memorised — <u>answer the question in the exam paper</u>. If you keep **referring back** to the question in your answer, then you won't get sidetracked.

• Keep an **eye on** the time. You'll lose marks if you spend an hour on the first question and only leave yourself 20 minutes for the other one.

At the end of the Exam

• If you have time at the end, **check through** your **answers**. Make any corrections **neat** and **obvious** — it makes it easier for the examiner to see your changes.

The Exam *Also* tests *How* you *Write*

You're writing for **someone else**, so don't make it hard for the examiner to understand what you're saying.

1) Structure your essay in **paragraphs** (see page 41).

2) Write in an **appropriate style**. This is a **formal** exam, so it's **not** a good idea to use slang, chattiness or text speak.

3) The examiner will consider your **spelling** and **grammar** when deciding the mark, so make sure your essay is easy to **read** and **understand**.

4) Use '**history terms**' which link to your module — e.g. **autocracy, Tsarism, Bolshevik**.

5) Write **neatly** — the examiner **can't give** you **marks** if they **can't read** what you've **written**.

You best be usin' proper grammar now — proper grammar is proper good...

If you didn't already know, examiners are not your friends — they're evil aliens from a far-away planet sent to make students' lives miserable... Anyway, the point is they're not your friend, so don't talk to them like one, otherwise they'll mark you down. Harshly.

The Mark Scheme

Mark Scheme — something that helps the examiner to figure out what level your exam answer is at so they can work out what mark to give it — and not the chief examiner's name. Easy mistake to make though...

Your answer will be given a **Level** from **1** to **5**

- Each level has a description of the **key features** the examiner is **looking for** in your answer.
- The examiner will try to **judge** which **level** your answer **matches best**.
- The examiner will then decide what **mark** to give you **within** that **level**. For example, if the examiner thinks that you've written a **high level 3** answer, then you might be awarded **18 marks**.
- Your **overall grade** will be **worked out later** after everyone's results have been collected.

This mark scheme is **similar** to the one the examiner uses:

Level	Description	Marks
1	Brief statements about the topic. Doesn't show clear understanding of the question. Facts are wrong. A few sentences and paragraphs. Poorly written.	1-6
2	Brief statements showing some understanding of the question being asked. Some facts are correct. Written in paragraphs, but poorly written.	7-12
3	Shows understanding of the question. Facts will mostly be correct. Events may be described rather than explained, or explained in little detail. It may not discuss points related to the question or only discuss one point without considering others. Written clearly and in paragraphs.	13-18
4	Understands the question and provides an explanation using well-structured paragraphs. Most facts will be accurate and used to support the explanation. Begins to reach conclusions. May not cover all the key points or the whole time period. Very well written.	19-24
5	Answers the question directly. The essay will acknowledge a range of factors and it will show an understanding of how factors and their relationships change over time. It will consider virtually the whole time period. Points that are made will be developed and clearly explained. Facts will be accurate and support the argument. The answer will reach a conclusion. Written and structured excellently.	25-30

Beat all the levels, rescue the princess, complete the exam.

My best friends — Mark Scheme, Natalie Curriculum and Keeley Stage V

Basically, to get a good mark you need to answer the question. That sounds pretty obvious, but lots of people end up writing about what they know, and not what the question wants. Answer the question properly and you should go far...

How to Structure Your Answer

Structuring your answer will keep you focused on the question in the exam. Knowing exactly what you are going to write will also make your answer flow much better. Exciting stuff this, and it could save your life... probably...

A *Good Introduction* shows that you *Understand* the *Question*

Your introduction sets the tone of your essay. Give the examiner a **good first impression**.

1) Identify **how** the **key factor affected** the statement you are going to discuss.
2) **Mention** other **factors**, **alternative arguments** or other **reasons**.
3) Show that you **know** the **significance** of the **time** and **people/events** in the question.

Don't spend **too long** on your introduction. Leave yourself **enough time** for the rest of the answer.

The *Main Paragraphs* show your *Argument*

Your paragraphs need to be **clear** and **concise** so that the examiner can easily follow your argument.

1) Try to write **5-8** paragraphs.
2) Each paragraph should make a **new point** that **adds** to your argument.
3) Show **how** the **main factors affected** the **statement** in your **question**.
4) **Balance** your answer by showing how **other factors** were **more** or **less important** — or by making points which **argue against** the statement made in the question.

A *Conclusion* should *Answer* the question

A good conclusion shows the examiner that you've come up with your **own interpretation** of the question.

1) A conclusion is your **final answer** to the question, so it should **round off** all of your points.
2) **Sum up** the points you made in your main paragraphs. You can show how **each point** was **relevant** to your answer.
3) You need to make a **judgement**, e.g.

> which **factor** was the **most important**, or which **short-term** and **long-term** factors had the **biggest impact** on an event.

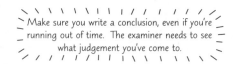

Make sure you write a conclusion, even if you're running out of time. The examiner needs to see what judgement you've come to.

In conclusion — planning makes perfect...

Plan your answer properly, focusing on the question being asked. Work out what your argument is going to be, and organise it so that there's one point per paragraph. And make sure your conclusion follows on nicely — it shouldn't introduce anything new, or go against everything you've just said — it should just be a nice summary of your argument and the points you've made.

How to Structure Paragraphs

Well-structured paragraphs are a recipe for success, but you could also try: a litre of cream, six eggs, ten tablespoons of sugar, a grating of nutmeg and a spoonful of treacle. Whisk it up and drink it down hot. Mmm... success...

Paragraphs are the **Building Blocks** of your essay

A paragraph should be **constructed** in the **same way** as an **essay**:

1) Make an **introductory** point.
2) **Support** your point with **explanation** and **factual evidence**.
3) Make a **concluding** point.

Jeff had two excellent points.

Each Paragraph needs to make a **Point**

1) You **won't** get many marks if you just **retell** the events. Like this...

When .... happened in .... war broke out.

Useful words for linking points

- Firstly / Secondly...
- Another...
- Consequently,
- Further...
- Of lesser importance,

2) Instead, your opening sentence should address the question **directly**. Like this...

The **most important reason** for the outbreak of war was .... because ....

3) Try to **link** your paragraph to the previous one so your answer flows.

Support your **Points** with **Evidence**

1) You need to **find evidence** and **examples** to **back up** your points.
2) You can then **develop** what you mean by giving a more **detailed explanation**.
3) Find **relevant factual evidence** to **support** the point you are making.
4) It's best if you can find **two** or **three** factual **examples** to **support** each point that you make.

End your paragraphs with a **Concluding Statement**

1) **Sum up** the point you made in your paragraph and **weigh up** the **importance** of the factor you've been discussing.
2) **Link** the **last sentence** with what you're going to discuss in the **next paragraph**, e.g.

This factor was important, but economic factors were more important...

Oh, what's the point of carrying on? Oooo — sample exam questions...

In a weird way, a paragraph is just like a mini essay. So your final answer will be an essay, full of mini essays... That's just confusing — forget I said anything. Let me start again. Write your paragraphs just like mini essays, and you should be fine. Much clearer.

Sample Multi-Factor Question

The most common type of question you'll encounter is the 'multi-factor' style question. This type of question will ask you to write about a number of different factors and how they contributed to a historical event.

Multi-factor questions ask you to think about More than One Factor

1) This type of question will ask you to explain the **causes** (or sometimes the **consequences**) of a **historical event**.

2) You will need to **weigh up** the importance of the factor in the question with **other factors** you have learnt about.

3) In the conclusion you'll need to make a **judgement** as to how **important** the factor in the **question** actually is.

Multi-factor questions will begin with phrases like:

- How far do you agree...
- To what extent...
- How accurate is it to say...

Highlight the Key Words in the question

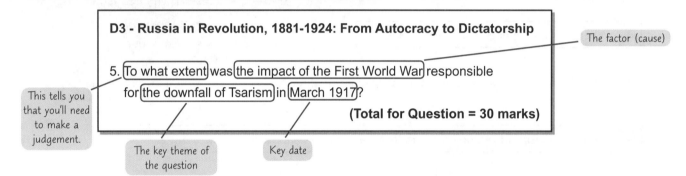

D3 - Russia in Revolution, 1881-1924: From Autocracy to Dictatorship

The factor (cause)

5. To what extent was the impact of the First World War responsible for the downfall of Tsarism in March 1917?

(Total for Question = 30 marks)

This tells you that you'll need to make a judgement.

The key theme of the question

Key date

Pick out the **important bits** of the question so you can work **out** what it's asking you to do:

1) **The judgement** — e.g. 'To what extent'. The question is asking you to make a **judgement** on **how important** a certain factor was in **causing** a certain **event** or **consequence**.

2) **The key theme** — e.g. 'the downfall of Tsarism'. The **focus** of your answer will be on how certain **factors caused** Tsarism to fall.

3) **The factor in the question** — e.g. 'the impact of the First World War'. The question will identify a **main factor** for you to look at, but it's **not** the **only** factor that you should **consider**.

4) **The time period** — e.g. 'March 1917'. The question focuses on **one moment** in history, but **long-term** factors can **pre-date** this event by months or years.

The Examiner wants you to...

1) **Explain** the **importance** of the First World War in causing the end of Tsarism, but **not** why the February Revolution happened (even though both things are connected).

2) **Compare** the **importance** of this factor with **other** possible reasons, e.g. you could mention the long-term **economic problems** in Russia, or **social inequalities**.

3) Make a **judgement** as to the **extent** to which the impact of the First World War was **responsible**.

4) Show how it was **more** or **less important** than any **other** factors.

How to Select the Right Information

By the time you get to the exam you'll have learnt loads of facts, but the sad thing is that you won't end up using most of them in your answers. Writing a good answer is all about selecting the right information from all the stuff in your head, and making sure it's relevant to the question. That's where these jolly pages come in.

Select the Information that's Relevant to the Question

The **factor** in the **question** is the **First World War**. So, the first thing you need is **evidence** that supports the idea that what happened during the **war** was the **main cause** of the **Revolution**.

You'll find this info on Page 18...

Events during the war meant that the soldiers were unhappy. This made them less likely to support the Tsar during the revolution.

① Armed Forces

1) **Millions** of men were conscripted into **large armies** known as the '**Russian steamroller**'.
2) Initial enthusiasm for the war was **shattered** by two early **defeats** at **Tannenberg** and the **Masurian Lakes in 1914.**
3) Conditions were **poor**. There were **insufficient food supplies** and a **lack** of **rifles** and **ammunition**.
4) Military **hospitals** were often **filthy** and had **insufficient medical supplies** — even bandages were in short supply.
5) The **military command structure** was **inefficient**. Officers were chosen because of their **social position** rather than their **military abilities**.
6) By **1916** the armed forces were **demoralised** and **undisciplined**. **Desertions** were common — even during the successful Brusilov Offensive over **50 000** soldiers deserted from the army.

The war badly affected the transport system. This caused problems for the army and also ordinary Russians who weren't getting food supplies.

② Transport

1) The **railway system** transported **troops** and **military equipment** — the needs of the army took **priority**.
2) The railways were **overloaded** in **peacetime** and by **1916** the system had **virtually collapsed**.
3) Armaments **factories** were producing plenty of **supplies** but the state of the railways meant they **couldn't be delivered.** Not enough **food** was getting through. Lines were **blocked** by engine failures and **grain** was left to **rot** in the sidings.
4) In **1916** food shortages were **widespread** and many people in towns were left **starving**.

These are all examples of how the war strained the economy, leading to more food shortages and greater unrest.

③ The Economy

1) In **1914** the government abandoned the **gold standard**, which linked the value of the rouble to Russia's gold reserves. This left the government free to **print** as many **bank notes** as they wanted.
2) This policy led to **inflation** — wages could not keep up with **rapidly rising prices**.
3) By **1916** peasants realised that because of inflation it wasn't worth selling their grain. So they started **hoarding** it — hoping for better times and **fairer prices.**
4) Russia's main ports for exporting goods were **blockaded**, which added to the government's **economic difficulties.**

... and on Page 19

Nicholas's leadership during the war made him look weak, so people lost respect for him. They didn't think the royal family was worth saving.

④ Nicholas and Alexandra

1) In September **1915** Nicholas II appointed himself **Commander-in-Chief** of the armed forces. He was **away** from Petrograd for long periods of time.
2) Nicholas appointed his wife Alexandra to **supervise** the **government** in his place. Because she was **German**, it was rumoured that she was passing **military secrets** to her German relatives (even though she wasn't).
3) Alexandra constantly **changed ministers**, causing **instability** in the government.

How to Select the Right Information

The points you'd use for this are on **Page 20**

You need to think about Other Factors too

1) The question also wants you to consider what **else** could have caused the downfall of Tsarism.
2) You'll need to show some **evidence** that the conditions for revolution were **already** in place **before** war broke out, even if you then go on to say that the war was still the most important factor.

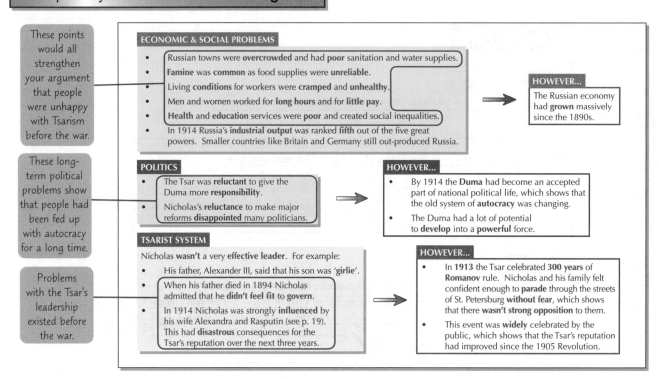

These points would all strengthen your argument that people were unhappy with Tsarism before the war.

ECONOMIC & SOCIAL PROBLEMS
- Russian towns were **overcrowded** and had **poor** sanitation and water supplies.
- **Famine** was **common** as food supplies were **unreliable**.
- Living **conditions** for workers were **cramped** and **unhealthy**.
- Men and women worked for **long hours** and for **little pay**.
- **Health** and **education** services were **poor** and created social inequalities.
- In 1914 Russia's **industrial output** was ranked **fifth** out of the five great powers. Smaller countries like Britain and Germany still out-produced Russia.

HOWEVER... The Russian economy had **grown** massively since the 1890s.

These long-term political problems show that people had been fed up with autocracy for a long time.

POLITICS
- The Tsar was **reluctant** to give the Duma more **responsibility**.
- Nicholas's **reluctance** to make major reforms **disappointed** many politicians.

HOWEVER...
- By 1914 the **Duma** had become an accepted part of national political life, which shows that the old system of **autocracy** was changing.
- The Duma had a lot of potential to **develop** into a **powerful** force.

Problems with the Tsar's leadership existed before the war.

TSARIST SYSTEM
Nicholas **wasn't a very effective leader**. For example:
- His father, Alexander III, said that his son was 'girlie'.
- When his father died in 1894 Nicholas admitted that he **didn't feel fit** to **govern**.
- In 1914 Nicholas was strongly **influenced** by his wife Alexandra and Rasputin (see p. 19). This had **disastrous** consequences for the Tsar's reputation over the next three years.

HOWEVER...
- In **1913** the Tsar celebrated **300 years** of **Romanov** rule. Nicholas and his family felt confident enough to **parade** through the streets of St. Petersburg **without fear**, which shows that there **wasn't strong opposition** to them.
- This event was **widely** celebrated by the public, which shows that the Tsar's reputation had improved since the 1905 Revolution.

This page also shows you how the **February Revolution** was **different** from the **1905 Revolution**. In **1905** the Tsar had the support of the **army** and the **wealthier classes**, but in **1917** his support **disappeared**.

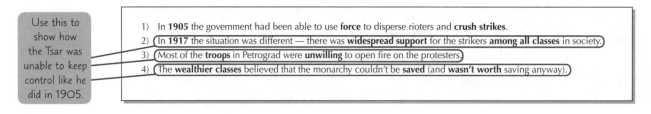

Use this to show how the Tsar was unable to keep control like he did in 1905.

1) In **1905** the government had been able to use **force** to disperse rioters and **crush strikes**.
2) In **1917** the situation was different — there was **widespread support** for the strikers **among all classes** in society.
3) Most of the **troops** in Petrograd were **unwilling** to open fire on the protesters.
4) The **wealthier classes** believed that the monarchy couldn't be **saved** (and **wasn't worth** saving anyway).

There is also some useful info on **Page 21**

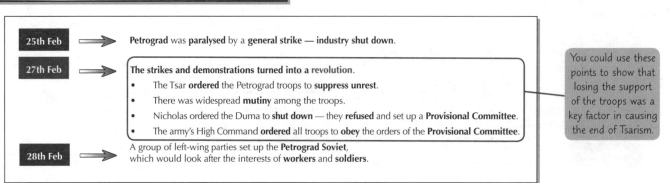

25th Feb → Petrograd was **paralysed** by a **general strike** — industry shut down.

27th Feb → The strikes and demonstrations turned into a **revolution**.
- The Tsar **ordered** the Petrograd troops to **suppress unrest**.
- There was widespread **mutiny** among the troops.
- Nicholas ordered the Duma to **shut down** — they **refused** and set up a **Provisional Committee**.
- The army's High Command **ordered** all troops to **obey** the orders of the **Provisional Committee**.

28th Feb → A group of left-wing parties set up the **Petrograd Soviet**, which would look after the interests of **workers** and **soldiers**.

You could use these points to show that losing the support of the troops was a key factor in causing the end of Tsarism.

How to Plan Your Answer

This page will help you plan for a multi-factor type question, like the one on page 42.

Use a **Plan** to **Structure** your **Argument**

Here's an example exam question to help show you how to write a good answer:

> To what extent was the impact of the First World War responsible for the downfall of Tsarism in March 1917?

You've only got **5 minutes** to do your plan, so don't make it too detailed.
Here are some things it could include:

1) **4-5 points** about how the First World War contributed to the fall of Tsarism.

2) **2-3 alternative factors** that might have contributed to the downfall of Tsarism (with **reasons why**).

3) Some notes on what your **conclusion** will be.

Link your paragraphs **together**

1) Think of ways to **link** your paragraphs together.
   Link points which are **closely** related, e.g. economic and social problems.

2) **Decide** which factor you think was the **most important**.

Your plan probably won't be as big as this. We've written it in full so it's easier to follow.

Here's an **Example Plan**

1. The First World War — Short-term factors
   * Early losses badly affected army morale.
   * Army undisciplined. Undermined Tsar's authority.
   * Huge strain on the economy — inflation led to peasants hoarding grain.
   * Transport system overstretched — supplies not getting to troops or towns.
   * Bad leadership from the Tsar. It seemed like he was controlled by his wife and Rasputin.

2. Economic Problems — Long-term factors
   * Economic reforms made life more difficult for ordinary Russians.
   * Russians worked long hours for little pay.

3. Social Problems — Long-term factors
   * Inequality in society. Health and education services inadequate.
   * Living and working conditions for many Russians were very poor.
   * Famine common. Food supplies unreliable.

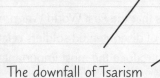

The downfall of Tsarism

5. February Revolution — Conclusion
   * February Revolution forced the Tsar to abdicate — ended Tsarism.
   * The Revolution — people lost faith in Tsar. Troops no longer loyal.
   * Decide which point most important — First World War or a long-term problem.

4. Political Problems — Long-term factors
   * Tsar reluctant to make any reforms that the Duma wanted.
   * Not prepared to give the Duma any responsibilities.

Worked Answer

These pages will show you how to take an okay answer and turn it into a really good one that will impress the examiner.

Use your **Introduction** to get off to a **Good Start**

These pages are all about how to word your sentences to impress the examiner, so we haven't included everything from the plan on page 45.

You might start with something like...

> Tsar Nicholas II abdicated in March 1917. The impact of the First World War was a very important factor in causing this, but there were other longer-term factors as well.

This intro is **okay** because it...

1) Says **what** happened in March 1917.
2) Tries to give some idea of **how important** the First World War was.
3) Suggests there were **other factors** involved.

However, it **doesn't** say what the **impact** of the **First World War** was. For example:

This also sets out different elements you're going to discuss in the main bit of the essay.

> In March 1917 Nicholas II abdicated and brought Tsarism in Russia to an end. The discontent of the soldiers, short-term economic problems and a lack of leadership during the First World War were all significant in creating the discontent that Nicholas faced.

You could show that you're going to talk about **long-term factors** as well:

It's good to point out what caused these problems.

> However, these difficulties were made worse by long-term social, economic and political problems which already existed because of the challenges of modernising the country. Together these problems contributed to the Tsar's inability to deal with discontent which was responsible for the downfall of Tsarism.

Make your **First Paragraph** about the **Key Factor**

> The First World War caused a lot of different problems. Russia lost early battles at Tannenberg and the Masurian Lakes. Shortages of food, ammunition and medical help meant the soldiers became demoralised and began to desert.

1) This paragraph **introduces** the **problems** that the First World War presented, and gives good **examples**.
2) But... it **doesn't** show how the problem of discontented soldiers **relates** to the fall of Tsarism.
3) To **improve** the paragraph you should introduce the most important point **straight away** instead:

This makes it much clearer that the war had an impact on ordinary soldiers.

> The failures of the war at the Front led ordinary soldiers to become increasingly demoralised. There were early losses at Tannenberg and the Masurian Lakes. Transport difficulties meant that the army couldn't be supplied with sufficient weapons, ammunition, food and medical supplies. Hundreds of thousands of soldiers deserted.

This explains why the soldiers were unhappy.

To really **impress** the examiner you should then show how this affected the soldiers' **attitude** towards Tsarism:

> Ordinary soldiers began to question the Tsar's ability to win the war, so when revolution broke out in Petrograd in February 1917, many soldiers joined in or refused to put down the uprising.

Worked Answer

You need to write about *Other Factors*

You might start like this:

> There were other, long-term factors that caused Tsarism to fall. The attempts to modernise Russia had created social, economic and political problems.

1) This paragraph presents **other factors** which **undermined** Tsarism — **long-term** factors.
2) However, you can make this paragraph **better** by giving some **examples** of long-term factors:

Good linking word.

> The attempts to modernise Russia made life difficult for ordinary people. Russian towns were overcrowded and people had to cope with poor sanitation and water supplies. Moreover, many Russians worked long hours for little pay, which caused great discontent.

Good examples of social and economic long-term factors that caused resentment among Russians.

This paragraph is **good** because it provides some examples of long-term factors, but you can **develop** this point by **linking** it to the **question**:

> The Tsar's attempts to modernise Russia had made life difficult for many people. Russian towns became overcrowded and, as a result, they had poor sanitation and water supplies. Moreover, Russia's desire to industrialise meant that people were forced to work long hours and for little pay. These long-term problems had not been solved by the start of the war, and many Russians blamed the Tsar for these failings.

This shows that there were long-term problems, before the war, that caused Tsarism to be unpopular.

You could *Link* some *Long-term* and *Short-term* factors together

You could say:

This identifies this point as a long-term factor because it refers to something before the war.

> Before the war, food shortages and famine were a problem in Russia. Stolypin had made some agricultural reforms to try to make Russia's farming system more efficient, but these reforms did not have enough time to achieve their aims. Food shortages made the people angry and resentful, and more likely to rebel.

This shows good knowledge of the period before the war.

1) Food shortages were a problem **before** the **war** — some would have **blamed** the **Tsar** for not tackling this problem.
2) However, during the war, food shortages became **even worse**, so you can **link** these points together:

> During the war there were food shortages in the towns and cities because food supplies were diverted to the soldiers. Furthermore, inflation, caused by the war, made money worthless and so the peasants did not sell their grain. This made the shortages much worse, causing starvation. These food shortages helped stir up the unrest that led to the revolution — and they were caused by both long-term failures in agriculture and the immediate impact of the war.

Good use of examples.

This links the long-term problems and the short-term problems.

When you **combine** these points together you can show that both **long-term** and **short-term** factors **undermined** loyalty to the Tsar.

Worked Answer

Link Long-Term and Short-Term factors to the Date in the question

It's important to show how the **factor** in the **question** (the impact of the First World War) has **combined** with **long-term factors** (economic, social and political) to **undermine** the Tsar. But to get top marks you need to:

1) **Link** these factors with the **immediate events** which led to the end of Tsarism.
2) Show an awareness of why the **date** in the question is important.

Something like this would work:

> A combination of the war and long-term factors led to the revolutionary discontent of 1917. These factors also combined to reduce the Tsar's power to stop the revolution once the events had got out of hand. Not only had the Tsar lost the support of ordinary people — he had lost the support of those who could have kept him in power.

Here you're linking the factors in your essay with the 'trigger' events that ended Tsarism.

Here you're stating what you think was responsible for the downfall of Tsarism.

You could **develop** this point by summarising why different people lost faith in the Tsar:

> By February 1917, the Tsar was in a very weak position. The army was unhappy with Nicholas's leadership during the war and with the poor conditions they were fighting in. The politicians in the Duma were finally convinced that after years of disagreement, they could not work with the Tsar. Furthermore, ordinary Russians were tired of famine, terrible living conditions and social inequalities which had been made worse by the war.

You've identified three important sets of people who were no longer supportive of the Tsar in February 1917.

Now you're showing how the long-term discontent boiled over during the harsh war years.

This paragraph shows how the **war**, **combined** with some **long-term** problems, caused the Tsar's support to **disappear** by 1917, leaving him **vulnerable** to a revolution.

Try to think Outside the Box — consider Wider Areas of Relevance...

You can **improve** your answer with **in-depth** knowledge:

> Discontent with the war and the lack of food led to a spontaneous uprising of soldiers and workers in Petrograd. In 1905, Nicholas had been able to use repression and political reform to fight back against a similar situation, but this time the Tsar did not have enough support to control the situation.

Reference to 1905 would impress the examiner — it shows you've thought about how the Tsar remained in power in a similar situation.

Referring to the **1905 Revolution** is **important** and **relevant** because that was **another** occasion where the Tsar had to deal with major unrest.

Finally, add some relevant **evidence** from the events of **1917**:

> Many soldiers felt sympathetic towards the protestors and so refused to fire on the demonstrations. The Duma refused to disband, and instead set up an alternative government, the Provisional Committee. Nicholas abdicated on 2nd March because, unlike in 1905, he didn't have enough support.

This is good supporting evidence to show how things were different from 1905.

Worked Answer

Finish your essay in Style

Your conclusion should **refer back** to the **key points** that you've made in each paragraph. If you've linked your paragraphs well then you'll have **created an argument**.

You could start with something like this:

> This is good because it refers directly to the factor in the question.

> In conclusion, the First World War was very important in causing the short-term discontent which led to the spontaneous revolution in February 1917, and in reducing the army's willingness to repress the revolution.

This is **okay**, but you can then **create balance** by referring to **other factors**. Like this:

> Good linking word.

> However, long-term economic and social factors had already created much discontent among the people. Furthermore the political activity of the Duma and the Petrograd Soviet proved that there were alternatives to Tsarism and autocracy.

> Using the correct historical terms will impress the examiner.

This is better because it shows you've **considered** other factors in your conclusion.

You need to make a Judgement

You **won't** have **answered** the question until you've made a **judgement** on which factor you think was **most important**.

You could write your judgement like this:

> This links back to the question and everything else you've written.

> Therefore, it was a combination of the war and long-term factors which meant that, when faced with the Revolution in February 1917, the Tsar was unable to overcome his opposition. This forced the Tsar to abdicate.

1) This kind of judgement is **fine**. It shows that you think **all** the **factors**, both long-term and short-term, were of **similar importance** in the downfall of Tsarism.

2) But, you can write a more **forceful** conclusion like this:

> Picking one factor over others shows that you've thought about your decision.

> The First World War was the most important factor in the downfall of Tsarism, because it made the other, long-term factors much worse, and robbed the Tsar of the support of the army — the key difference between survival in 1905 and downfall in 1917.

> This is a good justification of your choice.

This judgement is **better** because you've shown the examiner that, after considering **all** the factors, you've reached a decision on which factor was the **most important**. You've then **justified** this choice.

It doesn't matter what you decide — just make sure that you make a **judgement** and **justify** why you've made it.

Sample Single-Factor Question

Another type of question you might come across in the exam is the single-factor question. As you might have guessed, these questions will ask you to write about one factor or one historical event.

Make sure you **Stick** to the **Point**

1) This type of question is asking whether you **agree** or **disagree** with a statement, or whether something has **changed** or **developed** over time.

2) You might also have to make a **judgement** about an individual, action, policy or idea.

> **Single-factor questions will begin with phrases like:**
> - How successful was...
> - Do you agree that...
> - How significant was...
> - To what extent...

1) A single factor question may ask you about the **importance** of a **single** event, factor or individual. So you can either:
   - Write about the ways in which the **single factor** was **significant** or **not significant**, or...
   - Write about how the **single factor** was **significant** and suggest **other** more **significant factors**.
2) Or it will ask you whether a **single factor** has **changed over time**. So you should:
   - Write about the ways in which the **single factor changed**, and...
   - Write about the ways in which the **single factor stayed the same**.

Highlight the **Key Words** in the question

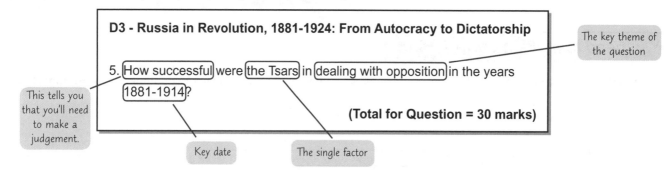

D3 - Russia in Revolution, 1881-1924: From Autocracy to Dictatorship

5. How successful were the Tsars in dealing with opposition in the years 1881-1914?

(Total for Question = 30 marks)

The key theme of the question

This tells you that you'll need to make a judgement.

Key date

The single factor

Pick out the **important bits** of the question so you can work out what it's asking you to do:

1) **The judgement** — e.g. 'How successful'. The question is asking you to make a **judgement** on **how successful** a single factor was in **causing** a certain **event** or **consequence**.
2) **The single factor** — e.g. 'the Tsars'. This is the **only** factor you need to **consider**.
3) **The key theme** — e.g. 'dealing with opposition'. The **focus** of your answer will be on how the **single factor**, the Tsars, **dealt** with **opposition**.
4) **The time period** — e.g. '1881-1914'. The question gives you a **long** time period to **find evidence** from, so **don't** look at anything **before** or **after** these dates.

The **Examiner** wants you to...

1) **Identify** the **different ways** in which the Tsars attempted to **deal** with **opposition** in **1881-1914**.
2) **Consider** how the actions taken by the Tsars were **successful** or **unsuccessful**.
3) Make a **judgement** about the **extent** of **success** during the years **1881-1914**.

How to Select the Right Information

Here's another set of lovely pages which show you how to select the right information for the exam.

Only Use the Facts that are Relevant to the Question

This page will help you pick out the **evidence** about **Alexander III's** methods of **dealing with opposition** that you'll want to use in your essay.

You'll find this info on Page 6...

It's important to remember that Alexander III's father was killed by radicals.

These are good examples of methods used by Alexander III to suppress opposition.

1) After Alexander II was assassinated, Alexander III issued the Temporary Regulations. They gave provincial governors and officials the power to **imprison** people **without trial**, **ban public meetings** and **exile** thousands of **offenders** to **Siberia**.
2) The **Okhrana** (secret police) **restricted** the **press** and monitored revolutionary and socialist groups.

Russification was an important policy to control the people.

1 Nationality

- Alexander III and Pobedonostsev promoted a policy of Russification (making Russia **more Russian**).
- In **1885** Russian became the **official language**. **Public office** was **closed** to people who couldn't speak it fluently.
- The rights of the Russian **majority** were put before those of minority groups.
- Alexander III **didn't distinguish** between minority groups who were traditionally **loyal** to Tsarism (e.g. Finns), and groups who **opposed** it (e.g. Poles and the Muslims of Central Asia).
- This **increased opposition** to Tsarism from many different sections of society.

However, some methods did backfire. Russification made Tsarism unpopular.

Some useful info about Russification.

Russia was a huge empire with millions of people of different cultures. Russification was introduced as a method of controlling them.

Land Captains helped the Tsar control the peasants.

2 Autocracy

- Alexander III declared that he was determined to **keep up** the **tradition** of **Tsarist autocracy**.
- In 1889 **elected** Justices of the Peace were replaced by the **Land Captains** — **aristocrats** appointed by the **Tsar**.
- Land Captains could **overrule** the **zemstva** (local council) and **charge peasant farmers** with minor offences.
- Peasants felt that the Land Captains treated them as **badly** as they had been during the years of **serfdom**.
- In 1890 the Tsar **restricted** the **right to vote** for the **zemstva** in the countryside, and in 1892 the right to vote for the **dumas** in the towns was restricted in a similar way. This gave the landed gentry even more power.

The Tsar tried to make sure that even minor political bodies wouldn't challenge his authority.

You'll find this info on Page 7...

Alexander III was successful in keeping opposition suppressed.

Summary of Alexander III's Reign

1) He provided **firm leadership** and a **clear direction** for the government.
2) He brought back **strong autocratic power**, underpinned by the **Church**, the **aristocracy** and the **army**.
3) He still had **opposition**, but it had been **weakened** and **driven underground**.
4) However, he found it **difficult** to tackle the **problems** emerging in his rapidly **industrialising** country.
5) He left a **legacy** of **repression** and **autocracy**, which Nicholas II continued.

The Tsar's failure to deal with this would lead to increased opposition in the future.

Nicholas wanted to repeat Alexander's success in dealing with opposition.

How to Select the Right Information

You need to **Remember** examples of when the Tsars were **Less Successful**

You'll need **evidence** of when the Tsars **didn't** deal with opposition effectively and why they were **less successful**. It's important to think about the **1905 Revolution** and the reasons **why** it happened.

You'll find this info on **Page 12**...

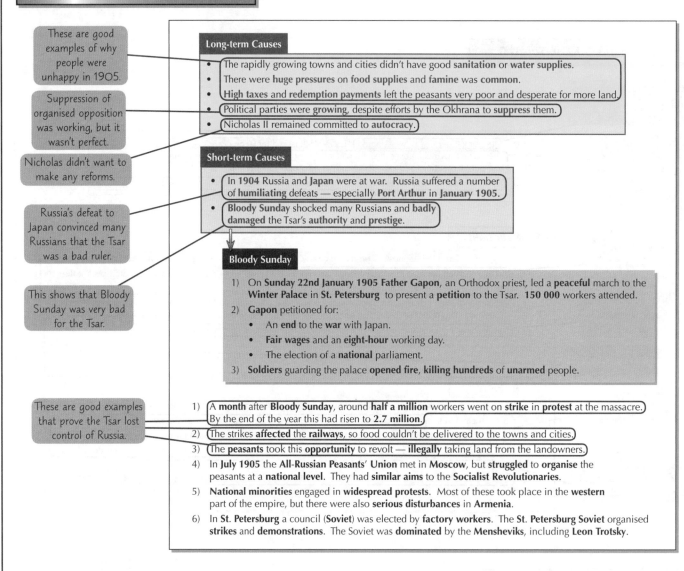

These are good examples of why people were unhappy in 1905.

Suppression of organised opposition was working, but it wasn't perfect.

Nicholas didn't want to make any reforms.

Russia's defeat to Japan convinced many Russians that the Tsar was a bad ruler.

This shows that Bloody Sunday was very bad for the Tsar.

Long-term Causes

- The rapidly growing towns and cities didn't have good **sanitation** or **water supplies**.
- There were **huge pressures** on **food supplies** and **famine** was **common**.
- **High taxes and redemption payments** left the peasants very poor and desperate for more land.
- Political parties were **growing**, despite efforts by the Okhrana to **suppress** them.
- Nicholas II remained committed to **autocracy**.

Short-term Causes

- In **1904** Russia and **Japan** were at war. Russia suffered a number of **humiliating** defeats — especially **Port Arthur** in **January 1905**.
- **Bloody Sunday** shocked many Russians and **badly damaged** the Tsar's **authority** and **prestige**.

Bloody Sunday

1) On **Sunday 22nd January 1905 Father Gapon**, an Orthodox priest, led a **peaceful** march to the **Winter Palace** in **St. Petersburg** to present a **petition** to the Tsar. **150 000** workers attended.
2) **Gapon** petitioned for:
   - An **end** to the **war** with Japan.
   - **Fair wages** and an **eight-hour** working day.
   - The election of a **national** parliament.
3) **Soldiers** guarding the palace **opened fire**, **killing hundreds** of **unarmed** people.

These are good examples that prove the Tsar lost control of Russia.

1) A **month** after **Bloody Sunday**, around **half a million** workers went on **strike** in **protest** at the massacre. By the end of the year this had risen to **2.7 million**.
2) The strikes **affected** the **railways**, so food couldn't be delivered to the towns and cities.
3) The **peasants** took this **opportunity** to revolt — **illegally** taking land from the landowners.
4) In **July 1905** the **All-Russian Peasants' Union** met in **Moscow**, but **struggled** to **organise** the peasants at a **national level**. They had **similar aims** to the Socialist Revolutionaries.
5) **National minorities** engaged in **widespread protests**. Most of these took place in the **western** part of the empire, but there were also **serious disturbances** in **Armenia**.
6) In **St. Petersburg** a council (**Soviet**) was elected by **factory workers**. The **St. Petersburg Soviet** organised **strikes** and **demonstrations**. The Soviet was **dominated** by the **Mensheviks**, including **Leon Trotsky**.

... and on **Page 13**

It's important to know what the Tsar promised in the October Manifesto.

The October Manifesto promised...

- Freedom of **speech**, **religion** and a **free press**.
- An **elected Duma** which had **actual authority**. **Laws** issued by the **Tsar** needed the **approval** of the Duma.
- In **November a second manifesto** was published. It promised to **improve** the **Peasant Land Bank** and to **abolish redemption payments** within a year.

These events show that the Tsar's promise of reforms helped him to regain his authority.

4) The October Manifesto **worked** and the **strikes** were **called off**.
5) **Spontaneous** demonstrations in **favour** of the Tsar were held in St. Petersburg.
6) The **St. Petersburg** Soviet was dissolved.
7) A **December** uprising in **Moscow**, led by **Bolsheviks**, was easily **crushed**.

How to Select the Right Information

You need to include evidence for the Whole Period

This question asks you to **judge** how **successful** the Tsars were in dealing with opposition in **1881-1914**.
So you need **evidence** for what **Nicholas II** was doing to deal with opposition **after 1905**.

You'll find this info on Page 15...

These are really good examples of reforms that the Tsar introduced to keep his opponents quiet.

1) The hated system of **Land Captains** was replaced by the **Justices of the Peace**.
2) There was a massive **increase** in **educational provision** for students of all ages.
3) **Political parties** which had been **attacked** by the Tsars and the Okhrana were now **legal**.
4) The debates which took place in the Dumas were widely **reported** and **discussed** in the **press**.
5) Nicholas II appeared to **change** his **attitude** towards the Dumas. In 1906 he wrote that he **spat** on the idea of a **constitution**, but six years later he wrote 'The Duma started **too fast**. Now it is **slower**, but **better**, and more **lasting**.'

... and on Page 16...

This shows that the Tsar combined reform with repression to deal with opposition.

The use of repression made many people resent the Tsar.

1) Stolypin was a **governor**. He used the **police** and the **army** to suppress unrest and keep a **firm grip** on his people.
2) In **1906** Nicholas appointed Stolypin as **Prime Minister**. By then most **revolutionary activity** had been put down, but there were still disturbances in the country, and **political assassinations** were happening more often.
3) Stolypin introduced a **new court system** where offenders were **rapidly tried** and **sentenced**. Thousands of rebels were tried, hundreds were **executed** and many were sentenced to **hard labour** or **exile**.
4) His strong measures were effective. By **1908** order had been **restored**, but Stolypin had made Tsarism even more **unpopular**.

Land reforms

Some good examples of reforms brought in to keep the peasants happy.

1) In **1906** the Tsar decreed that each peasant had an **unconditional right** to **land**.
2) They could **demand** their own **landholding** and farm it **without interference** from the **mir**.
3) Stolypin brought in **agricultural education** to train peasants in more advanced farming techniques in an attempt to **increase yields**.
4) He also sold vast areas of **Crown land** to the Peasant Land Bank for **resale** to the peasants, to increase the land **available** for farming.

... and on Page 17

Here are more examples of reforms that were introduced to keep peasants happy.

Other reforms

1) **Redemption payments** finally ended in **1907**.
2) **Internal passports** were abolished, so people had more **freedom**.
3) The unpopular **Land Captains** were replaced with elected **Justices of the Peace**.

The Tsar's combination of reform and repression did ensure that there were no further crises like the 1905 Revolution. But there was still unrest in Russia, and Stolypin was assassinated.

- Stolypin knew that his **agricultural reforms** would need to be **developed** and **established** over many years.
- But he was **assassinated in 1911**.
- Then **war** broke out in **1914**, meaning that the **long-term effects** of his reforms were **never realised**.

How to Plan Your Answer

This page will help you plan for a single-factor type question, like the one on page 50.

Use a **Plan** to **Structure** your **Argument**

Here's an example exam question to help show you how to write a good answer:

> How successful were the Tsars in dealing with opposition in the years 1881-1914?

You're going to have to find a way of **sorting** all the **evidence** into an answer that makes a **judgement**. You've not got long, so keep your plan **brief**. Here are some things it could include:

1) Evidence of **change over time**.
2) Notes on **periods** of **success** for the Tsars and **periods** of **difficulty**.
3) Some notes on your **conclusion**.

Link your paragraphs **together**

1) You need to think of points that argue **in favour** of the **importance**, **significance**, or **success** of the single-factor in the question.
2) You also need to think of points that argue **against** the importance, significance or success of the single-factor.
3) Decide on the best way to **organise** your points. You could **begin** by discussing all the **arguments in favour**, and then discuss all the **arguments against**. If the question asks about a **period of time**, you could order your work **chronologically**, putting the points **in favour** followed by the points **against** for each **key stage** in the period (e.g. for this question before 1905 and after 1905).
4) Select **relevant supporting material** for each point.

Here's an **Example Plan**

Your plan probably won't be as big as this. We've written it in full so it's easier to follow.

1. Successes before 1905
* Both Tsars used repression successfully.
* Okhrana suppressed Tsars' opposition.
* Land Captains kept rural opposition down.
* Alexander III used 'Russification' to suppress minorities.

2. Failures before 1905
* Repression suppressed opposition, but didn't deal with Russia's problems.
* Tsars failed to deal with main causes of opposition — poor working/living conditions, redemption payments and lack of land reforms.
* Political opponents exiled or imprisoned — not removed. Could return and cause trouble.
* Nicholas II's poor leadership against Japan (foreign opposition) made him look weak.

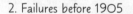
Dealing with opposition

5. Conclusion
* Russia under control, but problems weren't dealt with.
* Reform and repression combination was successful — but stored up problems for later.
* Tsarism weaker than it once was.

3. Successes in 1905 and after
* Nicholas regained control with concessions — October Manifesto and the Duma.
* Nicholas regained powers — Fundamental Law.
* Nicholas successfully used reform — Stolypin's agricultural reform, redemption payments ended, oppressed political parties legalised, Land Captains abolished.
* Repression — Stolypin's new court system — exiled or executed political opponents.

4. Failures in 1905 and after
* Repression backfired — Bloody Sunday sparked revolution.
* Concessions meant a loss of power.
* Nicholas broke promises — Fundamental Law.
* Problems with repression — Stolypin's brutality was unpopular.

Worked Answer

These pages will take an ordinary, everyday, uninspiring answer and turn it into pure exam gold. Oooooooh shiny...

Use your Introduction to get the examiner's Attention

You could write something like this...

> It's good to mention specific policies.

> Opposition to the Tsars grew in the period 1881-1914. Alexander III, with his policies of orthodoxy, autocracy and nationality, was very effective in dealing with opposition. However, Nicholas II was much less successful because he had to deal with a revolution in 1905.

This introduction is **all right**, but it's a bit **simple**. It **doesn't...**

1) Show how **complex** the situation was.
2) Mention the situation **after 1905**.

To achieve a **higher level** answer, you need to show how the situation **changed over time**:

> This shows knowledge of change over time.

> During the period 1881-1914, the Tsars were quite successful in dealing with opposition, mainly by the use of repressive methods. In 1914, revolutionary groups were not very active and support for the Tsar was steady. However, while Alexander III was successful throughout his reign, Nicholas II had nearly been overthrown in 1905. He had to introduce reforms to keep control.

Go on to talk about which Policies were Successful

You could start with this:

> This is a success for the Tsars, but you've only implied it. Make it more obvious.

> Both Tsars used repressive measures to deal with opposition. They used the secret police to spy on opposition parties, banned revolutionary ideas from being spread in public and sentenced opposition supporters to exile in Siberia. Many revolutionaries fled to escape the repression.

1) These sentences **describe** measures taken by the Tsars, but they **don't** say whether these measures **succeeded**.
2) To **improve** this you should **directly refer** to any **success** and show the **impact** that this success had:

> Success is clearly identified.

> It is good to have more detailed supporting evidence, like this.

> Both Tsars successfully used repressive measures against organised opposition parties. Opposition parties were under surveillance by the Okhrana and freedom of the press was very limited. Opponents who were considered dangerous to Tsarism were put on trial and were often exiled, and some were executed. These measures forced many revolutionaries to flee, and so they were unable to get involved in the 1905 Revolution.

> Here you've considered the impact this success had in helping the Tsars keep control.

Finally, you could go into **more detail** and point out some other **specific policies** which were **successful** in dealing with opposition.

> Alexander III had a number of successful policies to deal with opposition. For example, he created Land Captains, who enforced law and order over the peasants, and he introduced a programme of Russification, to promote Russian unity and suppress the influence of ethnic minorities in Russia. These repressive measures gave Alexander a firm grip on the country.

> Good use of examples and historical vocab.

This paragraph is good because you've provided some **examples** of **policies** which were **successful** in **dealing** with **opposition** and you've **explained why** they were **successful**.

Worked Answer

You need to write about the Tsars' *Failures*

To **balance** your answer, you should look at occasions when the Tsars were **less successful** in dealing with opposition.

This shows you're balancing your answer by thinking about when the Tsars were unsuccessful.

> The Tsars' methods of repressing opposition were (successful,) but the use of repression made Tsarism unpopular. The Tsars were also (unsuccessful) in dealing with the main causes of their opposition, such as the poor working and living conditions in Russia, the charging of redemption payments and the lack of land and political reforms.

This links the point back to the question.

These are good examples of things that created opposition in Russia.

This paragraph is **fine**. But you **need** to explain how the Tsars' **failure** to **address** the **causes** of **opposition** led to a period of **failure** against their **opposition**.

> Repressing opposition while failing to solve the problems that affected the Russian people meant that the Tsars were storing up problems for later. This growing dissatisfaction with Tsarism would come to the surface in the events of the 1905 Revolution —(the biggest loss of control the Tsars faced in this period.)

This shows that the Tsars' failure to deal with the causes of opposition in Russia became a big problem in 1905.

You should pay *Close Attention* to the *1905 Revolution* and its *Aftermath*

The **1905 Revolution** was a **crucial moment** in this period as it almost saw the **destruction** of **Tsarism**.

You could start by looking at how the Tsar was **unsuccessful** in **dealing** with his **opposition** in **1905**.

> The 1905 Revolution is where the Tsars' dealings with their opposition came closest to (complete failure.) Nicholas's attempts to use repression, which had previously been successful, backfired in the events of Bloody Sunday. Instead of suppressing opposition, (it made it worse) — following the massacre, strikes and protests forced Nicholas to change his methods.

This makes it very clear why the 1905 Revolution is relevant to the question.

Here you've shown that the use of repression wasn't always successful.

This is **good** because you've shown how Nicholas II was **unsuccessful** in **dealing** with **opposition** in **1905** and that this led to a **revolution**. You can **balance** this by writing about the **successes** Nicholas had in **dealing** with his **opposition** in **1905**.

> In many ways, the Tsar was successful in 1905 — despite all the opposition he faced, he remained in power. Nicholas had to agree to the reforms of the October Manifesto, which included establishing the Duma and legalising the previously oppressed opposition parties. Although this meant some loss of control, it pacified his opposition, and he himself later recognised that setting up the Duma was (a positive step.)

It's important to show that you've thought about how success could come in forms other than repression.

You also need to **evaluate** how **successful** the Tsar was in dealing with opposition **after 1905**.

Balanced points like these show how the Tsar was successful with a mixture of methods.

> The Tsar successfully dealt with opposition in the period up to 1914 by using a combination of repression and reform. Nicholas's Prime Minister, Stolypin, ruthlessly dealt with any revolutionaries, (but) also brought in agricultural reforms to address the concerns of the peasants.

> The Tsar clamped down on the more radical parties and repeatedly changed the rules for who could vote or sit in the Duma. (But) the Duma did make an important contribution to land reform and the provision of education, which showed that the Tsar could work successfully with some who had opposed him.

Try to make sure you cover the **whole period**, with analysis and examples of success and failure from 1881 to 1914.

Worked Answer

Make your conclusion **Balanced**

Show that you've thought about points both **for** and **against**.

You could start with...

> This point shows that sometimes the Tsars were successful.

> Alexander III was successful in dealing with opposition by using repressive methods of control. This quelled revolutionary activity in Russia, but it also caused great resentment among Russians and made Tsarism unpopular.

> Here you're considering that a successful method can have a negative long-term impact.

This paragraph shows that while Tsar Alexander III had **success** in dealing with opposition, his methods created **long-term problems** which would **affect** his successor, **Nicholas II**.

You could then add...

> This point shows that sometimes the Tsars were less successful.

> However, Nicholas II was almost overthrown by the spontaneous opposition of the people in 1905, and to stay in power he was forced to introduce reforms which gave liberal and democratic opposition more freedom.

> When making a point that suggests failure, you can link it to a point that shows success. The Tsar's reforms helped him to stay in power.

This paragraph shows that Tsar Nicholas had **less success** in dealing with opposition than his father. But it **also** shows that the **reforms** he reluctantly introduced were **successful** in **keeping** him in **power**.

Finish your conclusion with a **Final Assessment**

You'll get a **good mark** if you:
1) Consider the **whole time period** in the question.
2) Show an understanding of how the situation **changed over time**.

You could try...

> Alexander III was very successful in dealing with opposition to Tsarism, but Nicholas II had great difficulty in dealing with spontaneous demonstrations in 1905. Although the Tsar was able to successfully regain control, Tsarism was not as strong in 1914 as it had been in 1881.

> Here you've shown that things have changed over time.

This is **good** because you've made a **judgement** on how **successful** the Tsars were at dealing with the opposition to Tsarism, and you've shown that the situation **changed over time**.

You could **improve** this with more **detailed analysis**:

> The Tsars were successful in dealing with opposition, but their harsh methods of repression made many people resent Tsarism and didn't solve the main causes of their opposition. This became a major problem in 1905 when spontaneous demonstrations against the Tsar occurred, yet Nicholas successfully managed to keep control through a combination of reform and repression. He was able to restore the authority of the Tsar and deal with his opposition, but Tsarism was weaker in 1914 than it was in 1881.

> This clearly shows the examiner that you've made a firm judgement.

Sample 'Why' Type Question

The 'why' type of question is the least common type of question you'll come across in the exam, but it's still important that you know how to answer them. So, here's a page that tells you all you need to know.

'Why' questions are about Causation

'Why' questions ask you to:

1) **Explain** the reasons a **historical event** or **situation** occurred in the way that it did.

2) Make a **judgement** as to what were the most **important** causes for the historical event or situation.

Occasionally you'll be asked to consider **two events**, e.g. 'Why was X able to defeat Y, but not Z?'

Highlight the Key Words in the question

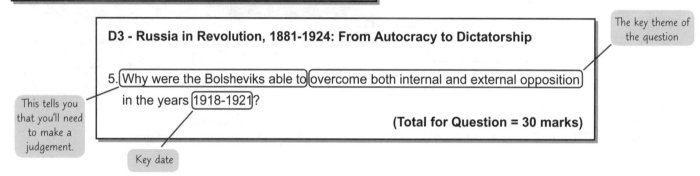

The key theme of the question

D3 - Russia in Revolution, 1881-1924: From Autocracy to Dictatorship

5. Why were the Bolsheviks able to overcome both internal and external opposition in the years 1918-1921?

(Total for Question = 30 marks)

This tells you that you'll need to make a judgement.

Key date

Pick out the **important bits** of the question so you can work out what it's asking you to do:

1) **The key theme** — e.g. 'overcome both internal and external opposition'. The **focus** of your answer will be on the **success** of the Bolsheviks in **overcoming** their **opposition**.

2) **The judgement** — e.g. 'Why were the Bolsheviks able to'. The question is asking you to make a **judgement** on **why** the Bolsheviks were **able to** overcome their opposition.

3) **The time period** — e.g. '1918-1921'. The question gives you a **short** time period to **find evidence** from, so **don't** look at anything **before** or **after** these dates.

'Why' questions can be **quite difficult** because they **don't** give you a **factor** in the **question** as a starting point. You have to think of **every point** that should go into your answer yourself.

The Examiner wants you to...

1) **Identify** the **internal** and **external opposition** to the Bolsheviks in the years **1918-1921** and the **different measures** used by the Bolsheviks to **overcome** their **opposition**.

2) **Suggest reasons** why the measures used by the Bolsheviks were **successful**.

3) Make a **judgement** about **which reason** was the **most important** in explaining Bolshevik **success**.

How to Select the Right Information

Here's the last set of mind-blowing pages which show you how to select the relevant information for the exam.

Select the Information that's Relevant to the Question

The question is asking you **why** the Bolsheviks were **able to** overcome their opposition, so you need to think of **evidence** of occasions when the Bolsheviks were **successful** in overcoming opponents.

You'll find this info on Page 29...

This shows that the Bolsheviks were willing to use force to overcome internal opposition.

The End of the Constituent Assembly

1) During the election campaign Lenin **spoke against** the Constituent Assembly. He argued that the **existence** of the **All-Russian Congress of Soviets** meant that the **Assembly** was **unnecessary**. Lenin also **claimed** there was **widespread corruption** during the election, but he had **no proof**.
2) The Constituent Assembly met in Petrograd on **5th January 1918** and the delegates held a **long** and **heated debate**. At **4am** on **6th January** the tired guards **asked** the delegates **to leave**.
3) When the delegates **returned**, later that morning, the **Assembly** had been **dissolved** on the orders of the government and the delegates were **dispersed** at gunpoint.
4) The dissolving of the Constituent Assembly was an **early sign** that the Bolsheviks **weren't prepared** to **share power** with any of the political parties.

... on Page 30...

This helps to explain why Lenin was so desperate to make peace with Germany — their foreign opposition.

1) Russia's involvement in the First World War had been a **major factor** in both the **fall** of **Tsarism** and in the **overthrow** of the **Provisional Government**.
2) Lenin knew that the **Bolshevik government** had to pull out of the war to avoid the same thing happening to them.
3) The **first act** of the Bolshevik government was to issue the **Decree on Peace**, which called for an **immediate end** to the **war**.
4) The Russian army **couldn't continue** to fight and Lenin ordered a **ceasefire**.

Lenin was prepared to **accept** such a **harsh treaty**, because Russia couldn't continue to fight in the war. He also knew that Russia might be able to **claim back** some of the land if Germany **lost** the war.

... and on Page 31

This shows that the Cheka was given great power to overcome internal opposition.

1) In **December 1917** the **Okhrana** was **replaced** by the **Extraordinary Commission for Combating Counter-Revolution and Sabotage** — better known as the **Cheka**.
2) The Cheka was far **more efficient** than the Okhrana. Its main **aims** were to **maintain state security** and **ensure** the **continuation** of Bolshevik rule.
3) The Cheka soon established itself **outside** of the **law**. It had the **power** to arrest, prosecute, imprison and execute **any real or suspected enemies** of the government.

Here's some important information on who the Cheka targeted.

1) In the summer of **1918**, **two assassination** attempts on **Lenin** gave **Felix Dzerzhinsky** (the head of Cheka) the excuse to unleash the **Red Terror**.
2) Thousands of Russians were rounded up and **executed** for anti-Bolshevik activity, including many members of **opposition parties**.
3) **Priests** were targeted as 'enemies of the people' in a sustained attack on the **Orthodox Church**. Churches were **looted** and **destroyed**.
4) Many people were **executed** for being **aristocrats** or members of the **middle class**.
5) In **July 1918** the former **Tsar Nicholas** and his **entire family** were **murdered** on Lenin's **orders**. Lenin feared that the Tsar could become a **figurehead** for the **opposition** to **rally** around.
6) The **Red Terror** came to an **end** in **1922**. It's estimated that up to **500 000** Russians died.

How to Select the Right Information

You need to look at the **Civil War**

There are **a lot** of reasons that **explain** why the Bolsheviks were able to **overcome** their **external opposition**.

You'll find this info on **Page 34**

This explains why the Bolsheviks' strong geographical position helped them to overcome the Whites.

Geographical Position

- The Bolsheviks only controlled about **15%** of the territory of the **old Russian Empire**.
- But this area was **densely populated**, had a good **railway network** and it included major **industrial centres**.
- The Red Army **wasn't spread out**. This made it **harder** for the Whites to find **weaknesses**.

It's important to know how War Communism helped the Red Army defeat the Whites.

Lenin's policy of War Communism made sure that the army was well fed and supplied with arms.

Leon Trotsky

- Trotsky created the Red Army almost **single-handedly**.
- He imposed **ruthless discipline** on his troops.
- Trotsky's leadership was **inspiring** and he raised the morale of soldiers when he visited the frontline in his armoured train.

These are good examples of why Trotsky's leadership helped the Bolsheviks to victory over the Whites.

Geographical Position

- The White armies were **separated** from one another by **huge distances**. They often were **unable** to **coordinate** attacks against the Bolsheviks.
- They **controlled** large **rural areas**, but were **unable** to gain the support of the **peasants**, who **feared** the Whites would **bring back** their former **landlords**.

This explains why the Whites' weak geographical position made it harder for them to defeat the Bolsheviks.

Disunity

- The leaders of the Whites **never worked together** to develop a strategy.
- The Whites **didn't** have a **common cause** — they only shared a hatred for the Bolsheviks.

The Whites' lack of leadership is another good reason why they were unable to defeat the Bolsheviks.

1) Russia's **western allies** in the First World War **feared** the **spread** of **communism** in Europe after the war.
2) They were also angry that the Bolsheviks had **no intention** of **paying back** Russia's **war debts**.
3) Britain, France, Japan and the US all sent small numbers of **troops** to Russia. They hoped this would **put pressure** on the Bolsheviks during the Civil War.
4) Foreign intervention was a **failure**. There was a lack of enthusiasm among the Allies for the conflict after the end of the First World War. Allied forces **never** made a **coordinated attempt** to **defeat** the Red Army. The troops were **withdrawn** in **1919** and **1920**.

This shows why the foreign intervention by Russia's former allies was ineffective.

... and on **Page 35**

Industry

1) **Industry** came under increased **government control**. The **Decree on Nationalisation** of **June 1918** led to **all** industry being **nationalised** (owned by the state) within **two years**.
2) **Private enterprise** was made **illegal**.
3) **Worker-controlled** factories were **abolished**, and many factories were put under their old management.
4) **Strikes** were made **illegal** and worker **discipline** was **tightened**.
5) During the Civil War, the whole **economy** was **geared** to the **needs** of the **Red Army**. **Non-essential** industries were **unable** to **function** efficiently and **output declined**.
6) The situation was made **worse** by a serious **shortage** of **manpower** due to the Civil War.

This is a good example of how War Communism helped the Bolsheviks overcome the Whites.

How to Select the Right Information

You should also look at Lenin's *Economic Policies*

For this question, you **don't** need to know every detail about the **economic policies** — you just need to know how they **contributed** to the Bolsheviks' **success** in **overcoming** their **opposition**.

You'll find this info on *Page 35*...

This shows that the Bolsheviks were prepared to be ruthless — War Communism guaranteed the Red Army was fed.

Agriculture

1) The government believed that **peasants**, especially the **kulaks**, were **hoarding grain** in order to **force prices** to **rise**. Lenin permitted the use of **force** to **requisition grain**.
2) Grain **requisition squads** went to villages to **seize** any grain they could find. Any **resistance** was put down **brutally** and many peasants were **shot**.
3) The forced requisitioning of grain was **unsuccessful**. Peasants saw **no point** in growing more food than their family needed. As a result agricultural production **fell steeply**.

... on *Page 36*...

This shows that the Bolsheviks used violence to crush the new internal opposition created by War Communism.

Tambov Rising

* In **1920-21, thousands** of peasants in **Tambov Province** rebelled in **resistance** to **grain requisitioning**.
* The rising was **well organised** and **effectively led**.
* It took **100 000** soldiers, led by **Tukhachevsky**, **several months** to **suppress** the uprising.

Kronstadt Rising

* In **1921, thousands** of **workers** and **sailors** gathered at the **Kronstadt** naval base near **Petrograd**.
* They demanded an **immediate** end to War Communism and **greater political freedoms**.
* Trotsky ordered **thousands** of **troops** to attack the base and the rising was **put down** after **savage fighting**.
* The **rebellion** at **Kronstadt** was a **symbolic blow** for the **Bolsheviks** because the **sailors of Kronstadt** had **famously helped the Bolsheviks' revolution** in **1917**.

This is good evidence to prove that Lenin was prepared to be flexible with his economic policies to overcome the new internal opposition.

Lenin said that the Kronstadt Rising was "the flash that lit up reality". He realised that War Communism **couldn't continue** in its existing form, so he **replaced** it with the **New Economic Policy** (see page 37).

... and on *Page 37*

The success of the New Economic Policy (NEP) explains why the Bolsheviks were able to pacify this new internal opposition.

The NEP was a **great success**. The Russian economy **recovered** after years of war, revolution and civil war.

How to Plan Your Answer

This page will help you plan for 'why' type questions, like the one on page 58.

Use a **Plan** to **Structure** your **Argument**

Here's an example exam question to help show you how to write a good answer:

> Why were the Bolsheviks able to overcome both internal and external opposition in the years 1918-1921?

Once you've remembered your **evidence**, you're going to have to **organise** it into an essay.
A plan will help you do this. You've only got **5 minutes**, so **don't** waste time.
Your plan could include:

1) **1-2 points** about why the Bolsheviks were able to overcome their **immediate opposition** after seizing power.

2) **2-3 points** about why the Bolsheviks were able to overcome **internal opposition**.

3) **2-3 points** about why the Bolsheviks were able to overcome **external opposition**.

4) **1-2 points** about why Lenin's **economic policies** helped to overcome **internal** and **external** opposition.

5) Some notes on your **conclusion**.

Link your paragraphs **Together**

1) Think of all the different **reasons/causes/factors** which will help you **answer the question**.

2) You need to decide how best to **organise** these reasons/causes/factors to answer the question. You could put them in order of **importance**, separate them into **long-term**, **short-term** and **immediate** causes or factors, or you could organise them **chronologically**.

3) However you organise your points, you must put together an **answer to the question**. **Analyse** the key points and come to a **judgement** — don't just write a list or tell the story.

4) Select **relevant supporting material** for each point.

Here's an **Example Plan**

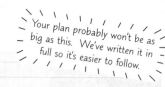
Your plan probably won't be as big as this. We've written it in full so it's easier to follow.

1. Immediate opposition in 1918
- Immediate internal and external opposition.
- Shut down Constituent Assembly — removed potential internal opponent.
- Made peace with Germany — removed major external opponent.

5. Conclusion
- Decide which of these points is the most important in explaining why the Bolsheviks were able to overcome their opposition.
- e.g. the Cheka — most important because it suppressed internal opposition.
- e.g. Trotsky's leadership — most important because he led the Red Army to victory.

Overcoming internal and external opposition

2. Overcoming internal opposition
- Created Cheka in Dec 1917.
- Summer 1918, began Red Terror.
- Persecuted actual opponents — e.g. anti-Bolsheviks and opposition politicians.
- Persecuted potential opponents — e.g. priests and aristocracy.
- Crushed opponents through violence and fear.

3. Overcoming external opposition
- Civil War — Bolshevik advantages over Whites.
- Better leadership — Trotsky.
- Better fed/equipped army — War Communism.
- Better geographical position.
- More united.

4. Economic policies
- War Communism helped to overcome external opposition — won Civil War.
- War Communism created internal opposition — used violence to suppress peasants and Kronstadt.
- Lenin showed flexibility, changed economic policy.
- NEP successfully pacified internal opposition.

Worked Answer

Ahh... we're almost finished, but before I go, here are some more pages that will help you to improve your essays.

A good **Introduction** will **Guide** your essay

You could start with:

Good use of historical vocab.

> There were many reasons why the Bolsheviks overcame both internal and external opposition in the years 1918 to 1921. The Bolsheviks were organised and ruthless, and their opposition was weak. This meant the Reds were able to defeat the Whites.

This intro is okay because it:
1) **Focuses** on the **question**.
2) Suggests **some reasons** that explain why the Bolsheviks **overcame** their **opposition**.

However, it's a bit **vague** and it **only** really focuses on the **Civil War**.
A **better** introduction would include more **detail**, like this:

This shows you're not focusing only on the Civil War.

Here you've identified reasons that explain the Bolshevik success.

> In 1918-1921, the Bolsheviks faced threats from opposition both inside and outside of Bolshevik-controlled Russia. In 1918, the Bolsheviks were able to remove opposing political parties and to make peace with the Germans. To consolidate their power, the Bolsheviks used terror as a method of suppressing internal opposition. However, Russia descended into civil war and the Bolsheviks were faced with several external opponents. By 1921, the Bolsheviks had succeeded in overcoming this opposition because they had a geographical advantage over their opponents, better organisation, unity and strong leadership.

You could start by looking at what the Bolsheviks did **First**

You could begin with:

> In January 1918 the Bolsheviks shut down the newly elected Constituent Assembly, and in March they made peace with the Germans. By doing this, the Bolsheviks were able to overcome their most pressing internal and external opposition.

1) These sentences **describe** what the **Bolsheviks** did to overcome their **internal** and **external** threats in early 1918, but they **don't** explain **why** they were successful in overcoming their opposition.
2) To **improve** this you should give some **reasons** to **explain** why the Bolsheviks were successful.

Here you're giving reasons why the Bolsheviks were able to deal with these threats.

> The Bolsheviks were successful in silencing early political opposition, because they were prepared to use force ruthlessly. They were not the biggest party in the newly elected Constituent Assembly, so in January 1918 Lenin used soldiers to shut it down. This removed one opponent to Bolshevik domination of Russia. But it was the Bolsheviks' willingness to make peace that took away their biggest external threat — Lenin made the decision to end the war with Germany. He knew the Russian people were desperate for peace, so he agreed to end the war, despite knowing that the peace treaty would be harsh.

This is **better** because you've **explained why** the Bolsheviks were able to **overcome** the **early opposition** they faced before they had fully secured their grip on power.

Worked Answer

Look at how the Bolsheviks overcame *Internal Opposition*

You could start with:

> In December 1917 the Bolsheviks created the Cheka to maintain state security. It had the power to arrest, prosecute, imprison or execute people. In 1918 Felix Dzerzhinsky, the head of the Cheka, unleashed the Red Terror, which caused the deaths of thousands of Russians.

It's good to give the names of important people. But make sure you can spell them.

This introduces the idea that the Bolsheviks used **violence and repression** to overcome **internal opposition**, but it **doesn't** provide any **details** as to whether this measure was successful or **why** it was successful.

To **improve** this you could write:

Here you've explained how these measures helped the Bolsheviks overcome their internal opposition.

> The Bolsheviks used terror to silence internal opposition. They created the Cheka (secret police) in 1917 which was responsible for the Red Terror — the imprisonment and execution of thousands of anti-Bolsheviks including members of opposition parties.
> The Cheka also persecuted people who were a potential threat to the Bolsheviks, such as priests, aristocrats and the middle class. This campaign of terror meant that much of their potential opposition was either destroyed by the Cheka or too afraid to speak out.

Look at how the Bolsheviks overcame *External Opposition*

During the **Civil War** the Bolsheviks overcame several **external threats** and you need to explain **why** they were **successful**.

You could start with:

> One reason why the Bolsheviks were able to overcome the Whites and their foreign allies in the Civil War was that they had a geographical advantage over them.

Using these words shows that you're answering the question.

This sentence introduces a **relevant** factor that **explains** the Bolsheviks' **success** in overcoming **external opposition**, but you could **improve** it by: 1)   Stating the **importance** of the **factor**.

2)   **Explaining** how it made the Bolsheviks **more able** to overcome their opponents.

You could write...

Here you've shown how important you think this factor was.

You've explained how this factor made the Bolsheviks more able to overcome their opposition.

> One of the most important underlying reasons why the Bolsheviks were able to overcome the Whites and their foreign allies was that they had a superior geographical position. The Bolsheviks controlled the most populated area of Russia and the main transport networks. In contrast, the Whites and their allies were spread across rural areas of Russia, making it difficult for them to coordinate attacks.

If you've found **a lot** of **reasons** why the Bolsheviks were able to **overcome** external opposition during the **Civil War**, then you should try to **link** these points **together**, rather than simply listing them.

For example, you could write something like this:

Link to the previous point.

This shows the importance of this factor.

> The geographical position of the Bolsheviks gave them advantages over the Whites and their foreign allies, and these advantages were turned into victories by the leadership of Leon Trotsky. Trotsky was crucial in inspiring the Bolsheviks to victory in the battlefield.

Introduction to the new point.

You could then go on to discuss why Trotsky was an important factor in the Bolsheviks' success.

Worked Answer

Make sure you cover the Whole Period

Don't forget to write about the Bolsheviks' **economic policies** which **helped** them **overcome** their **opposition**. You could write:

> The Bolsheviks introduced War Communism to ensure their troops got enough food and equipment to win the war against the Whites and their allies. War Communism was successful in helping the Red Army, but it created internal opposition because it caused starvation among civilians. Lenin introduced the New Economic Policy to keep the people happy.

Showing that a method used to defeat external opposition actually created internal opposition demonstrates a high level of analysis.

This paragraph is **fine** because it shows that the **economic policies** introduced by the Bolsheviks helped to overcome **internal** and **external** opposition, but it would be **better** if it was **linked** to the question.

An improvement would be:

> One of the key factors in the Bolsheviks' success against their opposition was War Communism which ensured their troops had enough food and equipment to defeat the Whites and their allies. However, while War Communism contributed to the Bolshevik success in overcoming their external opponents it also created strong internal opposition because it caused starvation and inflation. At first this opposition was ruthlessly suppressed, but after the Kronstadt Rising Lenin showed great flexibility. He introduced the New Economic Policy which successfully subdued this new internal opposition by ending grain requisitioning and relaxing the rules on private enterprise.

Referring back to the question like this shows the examiner that your point is relevant and that you're answering the question.

Decide which points are the Most Important for your Conclusion

You could begin by writing...

> In conclusion, the Bolsheviks were able to overcome their opposition because they successfully combined strong leadership and ruthlessness, and they exploited the weaknesses of their enemies.

This conclusion is **okay**, because it picks out some **reasons** which explain why the Bolsheviks **overcame** their **opposition**. However, you could write about how the Bolsheviks overcame their **internal** and **external** opposition **separately**.

You could write about how the Bolsheviks overcame **internal opposition** like this...

> The Bolsheviks were able to overcome internal opposition because they mixed ruthlessness and flexibility. They used force to shut the Constituent Assembly and to secure supplies during the Civil War. But when the reaction to War Communism seemed to be threatening the Bolsheviks, Lenin showed flexibility by bringing in the less strictly communist New Economic Policy.

You've made it clear that you think these were the strengths that enabled the Bolsheviks to deal with their internal opposition.

And about **external opposition** like this:

> The Bolsheviks overcame their first external threat by making peace with Germany. This vital decision meant they survived the war that had brought down both the Tsar and the Provisional Government. The Bolsheviks were able to defeat their later external opponents in the Civil War largely due to the many important advantages they had over their enemies. The Red Army was in a better geographical position than its enemies, it was better supplied due to War Communism and it was more united. However, the most important factor in Bolsheviks' success was the work of Leon Trotsky who created the Red Army and inspired it to victory.

You've made it clear that you think this was the most important reason in overcoming external opposition.

Then you can put them **together**.

Don't forget, you must make a **judgement** on which **reasons** you think were the **most important** in **explaining** why the Bolsheviks were **able to overcome** their **internal** and **external** opposition.

Index

1905 Revolution 5, 12, 13

A

Alexander II 3, 6
Alexander III 5-8, 20, 24
Alexandra 14, 19, 20
All-Russian Congress of
    Soviets 22, 27
April Theses 22, 24
autocracy 2, 6, 10, 12, 20

B

Battleship Potemkin 12
Black Army 32
Bloody Sunday 5, 12, 21
Bolshevik Central
    Committee 27
Bolsheviks 11, 13-15,
    21-37
Brest-Litovsk, Treaty of 28,
    30, 32
Brusilov, General 25, 26
Brusilov Offensive 18
Bukharin, Nikolai 37
Bunge, Nikolai 8

C

capitalism 4, 37
Cheka 28, 31
Civil War 28, 31-33, 35,
    36
communism 4, 11, 27, 34,
    36, 37
conclusion 40
Constituent Assembly 23,
    26-28
Council of People's
    Commissars 27
Council of State 15
Czech Legion 32, 33

D

Decree on Land 35
Decree on Nationalisation
    35
Decree on Peace 30
Decree on Workers'
    Control 35
Denikin, General 28, 32,
    33
Donbass region 3, 30
Duma 13-15, 19-21
Dzerzhinsky, Felix 28, 31

E

emancipation of the serfs 3,
    4, 6, 8

F

famine 5, 8, 10, 12, 16, 20,
    36
February Revolution 14, 20,
    21
First Duma 14, 15, 19
First Provisional Government
    22, 23
First World War 14, 18, 19,
    24, 25, 29, 30
Fourth Duma 15
Fundamental Law 14, 15

G

Gapon, Father 12
gold standard 9
grain requisition 35, 37

H

'how significant' questions
    50

I

industrialisation 5, 8, 10
inflation 18, 26, 36

J

July Days 22, 25, 27
June Offensive 22, 25
Justices of the Peace 15, 17

K

Kadets 13-15, 24
Kerensky, Alexander 22, 23,
    25-27
Kolchak, Admiral 28, 32, 33
Kornilov Affair 22
Kornilov, General 22, 26
Kronstadt Rising 28, 36
kulaks 10, 16, 35, 37

L

Land Captains 5, 6, 15, 17
land reforms 15-17
Lenin, Vladimir 11, 21, 22,
    24-31, 35-37
Liberals 23, 24
Lvov, Prince 22, 23, 25, 26

M

Makhno, Nestor 32
mark scheme 39
Marxism 3, 4, 11, 24
Masurian Lakes 18
Mensheviks 11-15, 21, 23,
    32
Military Revolutionary
    Committee 27
mir 10, 16, 17
Moscow Soviet 27
multi-factor questions 42

N

New Economic Policy 28,
    36, 37
Nicholas II 5, 8, 10, 13-16,
    19-21, 33

O

October Manifesto 5, 13, 15
October Revolution 22, 27
Octobrists 13, 15
Okhrana 3, 6, 11, 15, 20
Orthodox Church 2, 6, 31

P

paragraphs 38-41
People's Will 3, 6
Petrograd Soviet 21-23, 26,
    27
Pobedonostsev, Constantine
    5, 6
pogroms 7
Port Arthur 12
Progressive Bloc 19
Progressives 15, 26
Provisional Committee 21
Provisional Government
    21-27, 32

R

Rasputin, Gregory 14, 19, 20
Red Army 28, 32-36
redemption payments 3, 5,
    10, 12, 14, 17
Red Terror 28, 31
Russian Orthodox Church 2,
    6, 31
Russification 6, 7
Russo-Japanese War 5, 12
Russo-Polish War 33

S

Second Duma 15
Second Provisional
    Government 22, 26
serfs 2-4
Siberia 6, 17, 32
single-factor questions 50
Social Democrats 5, 11
Socialist Revolutionaries
    (SRs) 5, 11-13, 15,
    21, 23-27, 29, 32
Soviet Order Number 1 23
Stalin, Joseph 21
State Capitalism 28, 35
Stolypin, Peter 14-17
Supreme Council of the
    National Economy
    35

T

Tambov Rising 28, 36
Tannenberg 18
Trans-Siberian Railway 9,
    17, 32
Trotsky, Leon 12, 21, 22,
    27, 30, 32-34, 36, 37
Trudoviks 15

V

Vyshnegradsky, Ivan 5, 8

W

War Communism 28,
    35-37
Whites 28, 32-34
'why' type questions 58
Witte, Sergei 5, 8-10, 13
Wrangel, Baron 33

Y

Yudenich, General 28, 32,
    33

Z

Zemgor 14, 19
zemstva 6, 10